No Such Country

sightline books

The Iowa Series in Literary Nonfiction

Patricia Hampl & Carl H. Klaus, series editors

Elmar Lueth

No Such Country

Essays toward Home

University of Iowa Press Iowa City

University of Iowa Press, Iowa City 52242

Printed in the United States of America
Design by Richard Hendel
http://www.uiowa.edu/~uipress

The publication of this book was generously supported by the University of Iowa Foundation.

Printed on acid-free paper

Library of Congress
Cataloging-in-Publication Data
Lueth, Elmar, 1965–
No such country: essays toward home / by Elmar Lueth.
p. cm.—(Sightline books)
ISBN 0-87745-796-4 (pbk.)
1. Lueth, Elmar, 1965–. 2. German Americans—Biography. 3. Immigrants—United States—Biography. 4. Transnationalism. 5. Hamburg (Germany)—Biography. 6. Berlin (Germany)—Biography. 7. Iowa—Biography. 8. California—Biography. I. Title. II. Series.
E184.G3 L93 2002
973'.0431'0092—dc21 2001054278

02 03 04 05 06 P 5 4 3 2 1

FOR MY PARENTS

AND KAREN

Contents

Acknowledgments

For what they have taught me, for being friends as well as teachers, I would like to thank Carol de Saint Victor, Paul Diehl, Ed Folsom, David Hamilton, Carl Klaus, and Mary Trachsel. I'm glad to count among my friends Marilyn Abildskov, Michele Morano, and, of course, John Price. All of them gave generously of their time and insight. My deepest gratitude is to my wife, Karen, for her love and companionship.

My thanks to the editors and staff of the following journals, where four of the essays were published previously:

"Niemandsland," from *Sonora Review*.
"Word Choices," from *Gettysburg Review*.
"Houses," from *Bellingham Review*.
"Walk Don't Walk," from *Iowa Review*.

Introduction

Three days ago my wife, Karen, and I rented a truck and drove it to the Hamburg harbor. The harbor is one of the largest in Europe, and from a distance it looks like a city in itself. Tugboats, barges, and container ships make their way across the water and somehow manage to avoid each other. Behind them is a skyline of cranes, sluggish giants that handle everything from wheat to bananas to car parts. A few ships always sit in the dry docks, their names a study in foreign alphabets, their propellers suspended above water like sculptures. Here and there, welders crawl across their decks and ignite the air with flashes of blue light. In the far-off distance and almost swallowed by the city's haze are the flames of the oil refineries. In the foreground, surrounded by seagulls, the tourist boats wait for customers, filling at a steady pace, then disappearing into the dance on the water.

I used to go down to the harbor as a boy, listening to my father as he explained to me what I saw but only half understood. To come from Hamburg, as I do, means to know the harbor as the city's gate to the world, a place where the city brushes up against the promise of faraway countries. But three days ago, when Karen and I went to the harbor, we didn't come to sightsee. We had rented the truck to pick up our shipment of household goods — fifty-two cardboard boxes, a disassembled music stand, and an old, wooden school desk I hadn't been able to leave behind. Two months earlier, we had packed the boxes in our apartment in Iowa, getting ready for our move to Germany. The shipping agent from North American Van Lines had assured us that all our belongings would arrive in one piece. He was a tall, friendly man with a handshake that inspired confidence. But as I drove the truck into the heart of the harbor, through a labyrinth of roads and warehouses, a continent removed from where we had started out, I wasn't sure the agent's promise would hold. Our fifty-two boxes began to feel minuscule, the kind of shipment easily lost in the hull of a large vessel. I saw our boxes molding below some rusty deck, water soaking the cardboard until our towels and sweaters and silverware would quietly sink into the ocean.

My worries were unnecessary. The local shipping agent, who I found after a few wrong turns, knew of our shipment and sent us on to warehouse 59B. Here I handed my papers to a forklift driver, a short man dressed in a Hawaiian shirt, and within five minutes he returned, balancing the large, wooden crate I had last seen in Iowa City. Karen and I smiled, relieved. We didn't even mind that the crate turned out to be too big for the truck. We borrowed a crowbar and a hammer, took the crate apart, then used a hand truck to get the boxes loaded. It took us about an hour, and afterward we set out for the customs office. The officer who got assigned to our inspection was in his early thirties. Unlike his older colleagues we saw rushing back and forth, he seemed to have no need to let us feel the authority of his job. He waved us into the inspection area, cracked a couple of jokes, and climbed onto the truck. I was pleased that everything was going well. Another five minutes and we'd be on the road back to our house.

"Why don't you let me have a look at that box over there." The officer pointed to one of the larger boxes in the corner. I cleared away a path and cut open the tape. There was nothing for the officer to find. We had been careful to avoid anything that might be a problem—no food, no alcohol, no seeds. I didn't know what the box contained, but I watched without concern as the officer reached into it, his back toward us. When he turned around, he was holding in his arms a plastic cow the size of a small dog. "What is this?" he asked. Karen and I started laughing, which didn't help to explain anything. The officer held on to the cow, his eyes darting back and forth between us. "What is this?" he asked again, not unfriendly, but with determination. I told him that it was a lawn ornament, something people put up in front of their houses in the American Midwest. But the moment I started into my explanation, I knew that whatever story I had to offer wouldn't suffice. In the hands of the customs officer, the cow looked ridiculous, scratched and poorly made, the kind of thing nobody in his right mind would ship from one country to another.

The story I should have told, but that wouldn't come together in front of the officer, has to do with a visit to Belle Plaine, a small town in central Iowa. Shortly after we had met, Karen and I spent the weekend with friends who had moved to Belle Plaine a few months earlier. John and Stephanie were pleased to show us around, giving us a tour of the small downtown, treating us for lunch in the local diner. It was cool and pleasant out, and after lunch we continued our walk, drifted into the hardware store, pressed our faces against the barbershop window, and finally ended up in a five-and-dime. The place was long and narrow, lined with shelves full of pots and pans, plastic dolls, sewing kits, garden gloves, t-shirts, salt and pepper shakers, all of it jumbled together. I found the cow near the back of the store. Karen stood a few feet away, and since she wasn't looking at me, I stepped behind her and let the cow peek over her shoulder. She jumped and turned around, and then we both laughed, not so much because of my joke, but because we were still giddy with the newness of each other, the way our being together let the days slip by like water.

Months later, I took another trip to Belle Plaine, this time without Karen, and when John and I again set out for downtown, I told him we had to stop at the five-and-dime. I bought the cow for five dollars and for the rest of our walk carried it under my arm, ignoring the stares of passersby. I had decided to get the cow as a farewell gift for Karen. She was getting ready to move to California to continue with graduate school, while I had my own studies to finish in Iowa. Her decision to leave had been hanging over us for nearly half a year, something we had discussed like adults and agreed on as the only reasonable thing to do. But now that her departure was just two weeks away, being reasonable turned out to be harder than I had expected. We both knew that what we shared was worth keeping, and we worried about what the distance would do to us.

I had considered the idea of a gift for quite some time. I had debated whether to get a book and inscribe it so that the story it told would amplify our own, give it weight and direction before we parted. I had also thought about a necklace or earrings, something of value that would leave no doubt about our commitment. In the end, none of the ideas I had felt right. They seemed too eager, too filled with worry and anxious symbolism. And that was when I remembered the cow—its cartoonlike simplicity that almost meant nothing at all, except that it had once pulled us together on a good day and in an unlikely place. Karen liked the gift. And when she finally left for California, her Subaru groaning out of my driveway under the weight of her belongings, I saw the cow squeezed against the back window, framed by a sweatshirt and a stack of books. I saw it many more times over the next four years, which was how long Karen and I stayed apart, spending our money on plane tickets and phone bills, hoping that things would work out. When we decided to get married and Karen returned to Iowa, the cow made another trip across the country and ended up in our bedroom. For over a year, it leaned against our nightstand at a casual angle, studying nothing with its plastic stare and yet made more by the traces of story.

All of this I should have told the customs officer in the Hamburg harbor. And I also should have told him that Karen and I laughed because we took his find as a good omen, a hint that our life in Germany would come together, that Karen, who grew up near the stillness of Lake Michigan, would come to like our new home in time. But there was no room for such an explanation. When I finished my description of a Midwestern lawn ornament, the officer stared at me a moment longer and then pointed to another box he wanted to see. Ten minutes later the inspection was over. I drove the truck back into the city, fumbling my way through the gears, and kept thinking about what had happened at the customs office. It had been a minor incident, hardly worth noting, and yet it filled me with a sharp and familiar feeling—the sense of having two places to be, two stories to maintain, two selves to balance, and finding no easy bridge between them.

The doubleness I felt that day in the harbor is the kind of feeling I have slid into again and again since our arrival in Hamburg, whose bustle I left more than a decade ago to study in America. Even the house Karen and I live in for now has become part of this shift traveling through my mind. The house is the one I knew as a boy, and when I walk its rooms and climb its stairs, I find myself falling backward through the years until the time I have spent abroad is as light and distant as a dream. I notice this feeling most strongly in the basement, a room my brother and I used to play in and where I now have set up my writing desk. The room is a perfect rectangle with a low ceiling and two window slots. Thick water pipes run along three of its walls and come alive whenever someone takes a shower or does the dishes or rinses off a bunch of grapes. I come down to this room every morning, ready to begin my work, but then have to stop. It is as if, for a moment, writing in English were an impossible task. I sit at my desk and listen to the water rush underground, while the room around me remembers an earlier self, one that spoke only German, spoke it with the ease and certainty of a first language. All I can do is stay quiet and concentrate. And after a while I manage to free myself from the room's embrace, memory by memory, until I once again own English and with it that part of me I found in another country.

The essays collected in this book take an interest in such unexpected shifts and turns. They try to understand the texture of a home in motion, one that is marked by border crossings—both literal and psychological—and the intricate ripples sent out in their wake. Some of these borders are the ones I have crossed between Germany and America over the years. But there are also others. While living in America, I watched the country I was born in reunite on a small black-and-white television set in my study. I saw the long lines of East German cars inching through Checkpoint Charlie, their roofs glistening with champagne. I saw faces in the crowd unhinge and fill with disbelief. My mind flooded with images of an event I hadn't thought possible, and it proved too strong a distraction. So I packed my bags and returned for two years in 1991. I took a job in Berlin, began working in eastern Germany, and there found a new set of borders and behind them yet another way of gauging what is real.

Thus, the essays in this book move through a home that stretches across the three points of a triangle—America, western Germany, and eastern Germany. They retrace the journeys I have taken inside this triangle, stopping on a farm in California or in the streets of Berlin, wherever I found reason to linger and think about the dance of self and culture. Along the way, these essays have something to say about family, language, work, houses, and also the perplexing reality of history and memory. But their movement isn't toward resolution or the abstract clarity of argument. Instead, they move through a home that becomes more and more layered, following its constellations, telling its stories, and charting inside them the possibilities of belonging.

No Such Country

Kirchhoff & Sons

On hot days, the asphalt was like mud. Each time a truck pulled into the yard, its tires left the pattern of their tread like oversized fingerprints. Sometimes I sat right next to one of the soft patches and worked the asphalt with my thumb, making mountains and lakes and valleys. None of the landscapes I made stayed the same for very long. Filled with my geological powers, my thumb smelling like licorice, I soon discovered other constellations I had to try. Occasionally, I forgot where I was sitting, and I wouldn't notice the next truck coming in, wheels already turning to get through the narrow gate. Some of the drivers honked at me; others leaned out the window and yelled my name. And some, pleased to be back after a long tour, simply kept driving toward me, turning it into a game, wondering when I would look up. The rumble of the diesel engine would eventually bring me back to reality, and I jumped up, looking for the driver's face behind the windshield. We would wave at each other, and I'd step aside, studying the truck as it slid past, inches from my face, listening for the bottles rattling in their crates.

I was used to that sound. Most mornings I could hear the bottles while I was still in bed. The business was right next to our house, and when the forklift started moving pallets, loading the trucks for another day, the bottles would clink like far-off wind chimes. When I pulled up the shade in front of my window, I could see stacks of empty beer cases, three or four pallets high, waiting for their return trip to the breweries. There was also lots of empty mineral water, mostly Hella, which came in brown plastic crates—twelve bottles in a crate and forty-four crates in a pallet. One year, my brother and I spent a lot of afternoons climbing those Hella stacks. The company had started putting Hella-Points on their bottles, little colorful stamps that one could tear off and collect. Most people didn't bother with the points, and when the empty cases came back on the trucks, we would already be waiting, ready for our next harvest. A good day could yield fifty to a hundred points, which was a big step toward one of the prizes—large, shiny coffee-table books with titles like *The World of Super-Tankers* or *The Wild Kingdom of the Serengeti*. I never bothered reading the books. Sometimes I studied their pictures, but for the most part I just loved the way they looked on my bookshelf, like trophies.

My grandfather's office was right below our apartment, on the ground floor. He and my grandmother lived next door, and to get to work he simply had to circle around our house and climb the few stairs in the back. I liked to sit next to him at his desk and watch him add up long rows of handwritten numbers between puffs from his cigar. The best time to join him was late in the afternoon, when the office was blue with smoke, and the drivers would come in to deliver the money they had collected from customers. I knew all of the drivers by name, but I still felt shy around them. They would spot me next to my grandfather and make some joke about me being his assistant, ready to keep an eye on them. I could never think of an answer. Instead, I watched them pull their heavy leather wallets from their pockets and count out the money. Back then, in the early seventies, many of them still wore the traditional corduroy vest and pants, and underneath the vest a white shirt with sleeves rolled up above the elbows. They all struck me as men whose strength and purpose had no limits. They handled fifty-liter kegs like Mason jars, and they filled their hand trucks with more crates than looked possible, tilted skyscrapers they somehow kept from toppling. One by one, they filed past my grandfather's desk, and the cigar smoke mingled with the smell of sweat and sometimes the sharp sting of sweet cologne.

Outside my grandfather's office, right next to the stairs he climbed each morning, was the only place in the yard where disorder reigned continuously. Here the drivers could drop off their Müllkisten, crates they had picked up at pubs and stores that had the wrong bottles in them or crates that had tumbled off the truck and now contained only shards. Each day the place turned into a jungle of glass and plastic, and someone had to spend time beating it back. My father, who also worked in the business, was in charge of the yard, and he usually assigned one of the men to take care of it. Nobody liked the job, which made it easy for me to volunteer. After getting permission, I would start out by scanning the area for a couple of minutes, planning my approach. Then, I pulled apart the crates according to color and brand—a yellow stack for Holsten Pilsener, a green one for Ratsherren Pilsener, a red one for König Pilsener, and all the other stacks for mineral waters, lemonades, and juices. For a while it always looked like the chaos was getting worse, but once I began swapping bottles and throwing away trash, things started coming together.

My father would give me a pair of gloves for the job, which I took even though they didn't do much good. They were too large for my hands and kept slipping off. Instead of wearing the gloves, I stuck them into my back pocket, where they still managed to make me feel important. The only drawback of this approach was that I had to put my hands into the shards without protection and sooner or later ended up cutting myself. Sometimes I didn't notice the cut until I saw the dark drops of blood on my jeans or shoes. In the summer, working without gloves also meant I had to be careful around the wasps, which buzzed above the crates in thick clusters. They loved to crawl into the juice bottles and feed on whatever was left at the bottom. I liked holding the bottles in front of my eyes, where I could study the wasps' delicate frenzy up close and without risk, my nose touching the glass. When I got bored with the spectacle, and if there was enough juice left, I would give the bottle a hard shake and expel the wasp in a sugary tidal wave. The whole job, including wasp breaks, would take two or three hours. After I was done, I would hang around for a while, sitting on an upturned crate, sipping a Coke, waiting for the men to rush by and nod their approval.

Another place I liked to sit was the driver's seat of the forklift. We had only one then, a small red and gray Linde that could scurry around corners like a rabbit. In part, this was due to the ability of the driver, Herr Keitsch, who became part of the machine every time he took the wheel. When the yard was busy with trucks, all of them waiting to be unloaded, the forklift whirled around in circles, its engine a high-pitched whine interrupted by yells of "heppa, heppa," Herr Keitsch's favorite warning for anyone who might step into his path. If I got lucky, I would be able to slip into the driver's seat right after one of these frantic runs. The engine would still be warm, smelling of gasoline and oil. The rubber tires also had some warmth left in them, adding another layer of scent. I would grab the steering wheel with my left hand and let my feet dance across the pedals, while my right hand twisted the fork control like a twig. In my mind, there was nothing random about my movements. They were all performed with surgical precision. They were full of skill and confidence, and I couldn't imagine a better fate than growing up.

In 1902 my great-grandfather Johann Peter Christoph Kirchhoff sold his first few cases of beer in Hamburg. He was twenty-eight then, a newcomer to the city, freshly married and about to become the father of a son, Hans. Together with his wife, Anna, he sold beer, mineral water, and lemonade to a small circle of customers, using a horse-drawn wagon. The beer came from local breweries, but the mineral water and lemonade bottles he filled himself, each one marked with his name in thick, curvy letters. On his rounds, my great-grandfather wore a long leather apron that reached all the way to his ankles, a way to protect himself from the rough wooden crates and the inevitable spills. It took about two weeks for the apron to dry out and harden from the beer and lemonade, and when it was stiff enough almost to stand by itself, Johann would spend an hour after work oiling it, rubbing it back into smoothness so it would bend once more with his body, leaving him room to climb the wagon, to lift the crates and carry them to his customers.

The business did well. But in 1914 Johann was drafted into the army, and for the next three years Anna had to manage alone, reading her husband's letters from France over and over again. By now, there was a second son, Erich, who had been born in 1909. Anna wrote petitions to the chamber of commerce and to the military administration, hoping to convince someone to let her husband come home. None of it made a difference. So she pared down the number of customers and told her sons they had to help out, that this wasn't a game but something they had to do to keep the business together. Hans learned how to handle the horse and wagon, and since the full crates were still too heavy for him, he first loaded the wagon with empty crates and then filled them with two bottles at a time. When he pulled up in front of a customer's place, he did the same in reverse, unless someone came outside to help. Erich, seven years younger, could do little more than get in the way at first. But when he turned six in 1915, he started pulling a handcart along neighborhood sidewalks, delivering small orders to customers, who sometimes gave him candy in return.

Some eighty years later, Erich still remembered the moment his father came back from the war. He showed up without prior announcement, seated on top of a large horse-drawn wagon, dressed in uniform. According to Erich, the uniform was snow-white, lifting Johann away from the reality of the wagon, suspending him in midair like an apparition, which the boy understood as his reward for the hours he had spent with the handcart and bottles. Hans too must have been struck by his father's appearance, the older of the two sons, whose responsibilities had weighed on him more heavily, more consciously. Three years after the war, Hans joined his father as a partner in the business, and another six years after that, in 1927, Erich did the same. From time to time I have thought about the brothers' decision. I wonder whether it was just a pragmatic choice, a sensible thing to do to make a living with the familiar. They may have simply enjoyed the work. Or is it possible that there was something else—that the work had become colored with the chance of mending their father's absence, of restoring order to a world they suddenly understood to be broken? I'm not sure. Whatever the reason, Johann was pleased, and from then on the business had a new name: Kirchhoff & Sons.

In the thirties and early forties, additional men had to be hired, and the horse-drawn wagons made room for trucks, Hanomags and Dürkopps, machines that no longer took off by themselves to get home and rest. When the next war came, Johann was too old to go. His sons were able to stay as well, because they had begun to sell drinks to the cafeterias of companies that built airplanes and ships. But in the end, the war did find them. On the night of July 29, 1943, bombs rained down on Hamburg, and the business disappeared in fire—offices, trucks, filling machines, sacks of sugar, crates, and a quarter-million bottles. All of it gone in one night. With no time to let the loss sink in, to understand the unreality of having their livelihood swept away like chalk, Johann and his sons fell back to work. The day after the attack, they searched the rubble for anything useful, climbing hills of hot, broken glass, clutching handkerchiefs to their mouths against the smoke. And when that task was done, they combed through the battered city, looking for a place to start over.

It took them three months to find one, a few acres in Bramfeld, where our house would later be built next to the beer yard. The Office of War Damages paid out some money, and they once more started a stock of bottles and crates, bought trucks, filling machines, and the sugar they needed for their lemonades. Again the business grew, new men joined, and the trucks traveled even longer routes, sometimes outside the city limits. It is from this time on, the forties making room for the fifties, that the stories I know thicken—stories I would hear years later, during high school, when I spent part of my summers helping at the business. A lot of the stories involved the same protagonists, men like Otto Sorge or Kuddel Klug, whose capacity for work and drink, I understood, had been extraordinary. Six days a week, often seven, they drove their rounds, loading and unloading crates by hand for twelve to fourteen hours. The heaviest crates weighed around a hundred pounds, and the men called them "coffins" because they knew what those crates would do to their shoulders and backs. In those days hardly any of the pubs and restaurants called in their orders ahead of time. They expected the drivers to show up once a week, and then would decide what was needed. In this way, the drivers ended up salesmen who tried to talk their customers into buying more than they wanted. And to back up their sales pitch, they would promise to carry the crates wherever necessary, behind bar counters, into attics, and most often into poorly lit basements, some low enough to make them crouch, some teeming with rats.

The drinking was part of the sale, a ritual that couldn't be left out. Sometimes the drivers would get invited, but more often they paid for their drinks, hoping to lubricate the deals to come. Each of them had a daily allowance of five Marks for that purpose, and on most days that money would be spent. After nine or ten stops, it was impossible not to be drunk, and then it became easy to let a crate or two slip, the bottles exploding and washing down basement stairs like a river of foam. More serious accidents happened too. After all, the men would have to drive their trucks home through city traffic, and by then poor judgment came without effort. In one story, Otto Sorge overlooked a fire hydrant and snapped it like a leaf of grass. When he understood what was happening, water drumming on his cab, he climbed out of the truck and ran back into the restaurant he had just left. He dashed into the kitchen, asked for vinegar, and drank half the bottle in one gulp. The police, who arrived a few minutes later, asked a lot of questions, but they never noticed the alcohol underneath the vinegar. After half an hour, Otto Sorge was allowed to finish his tour. That was how most of the stories ended, back at the business, the work done, and whatever else had happened before somehow made right by that simple fact.

In 1954 Johann died, and Hans, the more quiet of the two brothers, took over the office, keeping track of the books. A few times a day he would leave his desk and check up on the trucks. After the death of his father, he grew into the habit of scanning the ground as he walked across the beer yard, looking for stray bottle tops that he would pick up, brush off, and slide into the pocket of his vest, like pieces of a puzzle. If the bottle top was damaged, the wire hood bent or the rubber seal broken, he would repair it carefully and then hand it, together with the good ones, to the man in charge of maintaining the bottles. Erich too spent more hours in the office now, but he still liked to go out with the truck. Unlike Hans, he had a taste for the pubs and the endless drinks. Years later, he told me about one of his favorite stops from this time, a small pub on Postweg where the owner always greeted him with a freshly poured Pilsener. The man never said a word to Erich while he drank the beer. He would watch from behind the counter, waiting for him to finish. When Erich had emptied the glass, the man would lean toward him and say the same thing every week: "Now pray, work, and don't be so lazy." Erich would laugh, slap his hand on the counter, and walk out to his truck. He would lift the first crate onto his shoulder, let the weight settle in his back, and begin his climb down into the basement.

Hans and Erich, now seniors, soon began to make room for the next generation. Both had married in the thirties, and both had two children. Hans and his wife, Anni, had a daughter and a son, Anneliese and Peter. Erich and his wife, Wilma, had two daughters, Frieda and Renate. Nobody expected the daughters to take an interest in the company, or even dreamed of encouraging it. All the attention focused on Peter. He became an apprentice in a machine shop, something useful and solid in Hans's opinion. For his final project as an apprentice, Peter made an oversized die from solid steel and mounted it on a wooden base like a statue. It later ended up in my grandparents' living room, where I would lift it off the shelf and always be surprised by its weight. When the apprenticeship ended, Peter came into the business, studying the patterns of trucks and men, learning to accept the pull of the crates.

But he wasn't the only one to do so. In 1957 Anneliese married my father, Horst Lueth, and two years later he too became part of Kirchhoff & Sons. As if to mark my father's entry into this circle of men, the summer he joined turned out to be one of the hottest on record. People drank all day long to make the heat bearable, and the stores and pubs called in with orders day and night. When they couldn't get through on the phone, they sent telegrams begging for a truck to come by. Soon a lot of the men, including my father, didn't bother to go home anymore. They started working at three or four in the morning, loading the trucks when it was still cool. Then the trucks would travel out into the city, coming and going for the next fifteen hours, their springs flat and stiff from overuse. At night, when the last truck returned, the filling machines would still be going, bottles tinkling in different keys as they grew heavy with mineral water and lemonade. Next to the filling machines, some of the men sat with tubs and brushes to clean the bottles that had come back late in the day, preparing them for the next morning. Around midnight, the air cool once more, Hans would finally turn off the machines, and in the sudden silence my father and the others would grab some blankets and curl up on the floor.

It is odd for me to write about the summer of 1959 and the history that came before it. I can't quite rid myself of the feeling that the words I use are insufficient, too light to capture the weight of the crates, the long hours spent driving the horse-drawn wagons and the trucks. I know this feeling has something to do with my choice to make words my livelihood, and not, like my brother, the rituals of our family business. What heightens this feeling of remove is the fact that the words I use belong to another country, America, where I make my home for now. But it is the work of my family I want to think about, and so I have to try to make the words do what they can.

Going over the stories of the business, looking for a way to make them come together, I keep returning to Erich and the pub on Postweg, where more than forty years ago a man would lean across a counter and say the same words every week. "Pray, work, and don't be so lazy." Words again. What strikes me is the imbalance of that sentence, the way prayer pales next to the double embrace of work. I say that sentence out loud, and I can hear the idea of prayer bending, following the pull of the other words until it is inside them, until work itself carries the promise of redemption. And then the stories I have about Johann and his sons, Otto Sorge and the other drivers, and also my father begin to add up to a portrait of men who believed this promise, who relied on work to guide them through loss, the ravages of war, the failings of their bodies.

At the end of his first summer in the business, my father had lost sixteen pounds. I know from pictures that he had no weight to spare. In his twenties, he was slender, almost skinny, and the loss of those pounds must have made his shoulder blades stand out like wings. His efforts that summer earned him Hans's confidence, who never after doubted the decision to let his son-in-law join. My father in return liked working for Hans. He accepted his judgment and took his advice. The two men learned to respect each other as they kept the business alive, spending whatever hours they thought necessary to get the work done. But I believe now there might have been something else that pulled them together, not just the work, but an unspoken recognition of what the work was meant to accomplish on the inside.

When my father came into the business, his own father had been dead twelve years. Albert Lueth had died March 17, 1947, on his way to work. As always he had come to the Hamburg harbor that day and jumped on the boat to take him to the Blohm & Voß shipyards, where he held a job as a machinist. It was a short ride across the river, but that morning the boat never reached its destination. The captain dozed off at the helm, and, in the uncertain light of early morning, the boat was rammed by a tanker unable to change course. Albert and three other men were thrown overboard and within minutes drowned in the still icy water. Six weeks later, Albert's body surfaced downstream, and by then my father's life had changed more completely than he could have imagined. He was fourteen, the oldest of three children, and less than a month after the accident he left school to help his mother get by. Albert's company was eager to assist the family, and so my father ended up an apprentice at Blohm & Voß, surrounded by the men who had worked with Albert, who now placed their hands on his shoulders and guided him into his father's craft. It must have seemed like a dark dream to the boy to be in his father's place, to fill his father's leaving each day with his own body as he got up, came down to the harbor, and stepped onto the boat. He must have worried that whatever he did wouldn't be enough.

I put this story next to the one I have about Hans, the three years he helped run the business while his father fought in France, a boy of twelve sliding bottles into crates too heavy to lift, and I see the similarity, the way both boys fell into their fathers' world before they were ready, before they could understand that they should not attempt and would not achieve such a transformation. Maybe I'm making too much of this, looking for symmetry in the stories with the hunger of hindsight. Hans's loss wasn't permanent, he had a lifetime to spend alongside his father. But three years stretch differently through the mind of a twelve-year-old than they do through the mind of someone older, and so I trust the connection I see is more than an invention. Hans and his son-in-law grew close in 1959, and they stayed close for the next twenty years, outlasting Erich, who retired in 1964 after a quarrel with his brother. And they also, more unexpectedly, outlasted Hans's son, Peter, who after he had come into the business didn't find much to hold him. He felt no passion for the work, and whenever he had the choice between another hour at the filling machine or an hour with friends, he chose the latter. He left the business in the seventies, taking his share in cash and beginning a string of jobs, none of which he would keep for very long.

Like Hans, my father expected the drivers to make it through their tours, and as long as they did, he too was willing to overlook other problems. If one of them overslept, still groggy with drink, he would start a string of wake-up calls until the man crawled out of bed and answered. If that didn't help, he would sometimes get in his car and pay a visit, pulling the driver out of bed, gathering his clothes, and sending him into a cold shower. On the way back to the business, he would stop at a bakery for rolls and coffee, making sure the man had his breakfast and a little more time to wake up and get ready. There were other ways too in which my father took care of the drivers. He gave them free credit when they were short on money near the end of the month, having miscalculated their expenses or simply having stayed too long at a card game that refused to go their way. Most of the credits were small, but some were substantial, money meant to help with new furniture or a down payment on a car. If a driver fell ill and had to go to the hospital, my father was sure to visit. And once, I remember, he served as a go-between in the midst of a marital crisis. My father performed these acts willingly, generous with his time, but it was always clear that he did so within a set of rules that couldn't change. The men deserved his attention because they were loyal, ready to work long hours without serious complaint. If one of the men, as sometimes happened, complained in earnest and began to take shortcuts through his day, avoiding the work and finding excuses, my father soon lost interest. Even though there might not be enough reason to let such a man go, he would, in the sharp light of my father's vision, become invisible.

Both my brother and I began to help out in the business in high school. It was a summer job we didn't have to apply for, and the money we earned paid for our latest obsessions, a new bicycle or maybe a complete set of Beatles albums. My brother, who is four years older, started into this work well ahead of me, and I envied his ability to move among the men with purpose. On a few occasions he was allowed to accompany one of the drivers, which impressed me even more, leaving no doubt in my mind that my brother had slipped out of reach and into adulthood. After work he would come home exhausted and take a hot bath before dinner. I waited for him and sat down next to the tub, asking him questions about what he had done and seen. He groaned and told me to shut up. But I didn't. I repeated my questions until he relented, until he gave me at least a few details. Then I sat in silence, watching him move his arms, legs, and shoulders, wondering when mine would measure up to his.

I was sixteen when I had my first full-time stint in the business, and I quickly learned what my brother had found so attractive about the hot baths. The work surprised me. It emptied me out in a couple of days, and I spent most of the evenings dozing on the living room floor, hoping I would hear the alarm clock the next morning. It also taught me to see my father's daily routine in a new light. I had been impatient with the monotony of his evenings, which included nothing but three or four silent hours of television. On Saturdays, he seemed to wake up to the memory of other possibilities, a trip to the local pool or a walk in the woods. But by Sunday he was back in front of the television, silent and distracted, the next week hanging over him like gauze. After I started working, I began to understand why my father could let his days slip by like that, frozen into slow motion in his armchair. His life made a clearer kind of sense. But my understanding also scared me. At sixteen, I wanted above anything else to fall into whatever experience could be had. I didn't want to think about limiting my hunger for friends, for traveling, for the odd ideas I picked up in novels. And yet, the reality of the work, its absolute claim on my body, seemed to hint at the possibility that such things could be lost.

During the weeks I helped out, my father was pleased to have me in the business. He joked with me when we ran into each other in the yard, and at the end of the day he sent me home almost tenderly, putting a hand on my shoulder, telling me to get some rest. These were the moments, I think, when he came closest to saying something about love, a word he shied away from, as if it could push him into terrain too uncertain for the grasp of his hands. I was eager for his attention in those moments, sensing the depth of what remained unsaid. And I worked hard. I ignored my tiredness and rushed my hand truck back and forth between pallets, putting together orders that would go out on the trucks the next day. A few times I overloaded the hand truck and lost control, six or seven crates crashing around my feet. It made a terrible noise, and I rushed off to get a broom to sweep away my embarrassment.

I liked how the work almost made me a peer among the drivers. How it made me a part of my father's world. And although I resisted the way the work numbed and exhausted me, I discovered that there was another payoff I hadn't expected. It straightened my days into a solid track on which it seemed much harder to derail than before. My worries about school, my awkwardness around girls, and the nagging question of who I planned to be felt less urgent. The work contained me and held out the promise of continuing to do so, if I only gave in to it all the way. I caught a glimpse back then, I believe, of what the work meant to my father and the other men. But when my time was up after four weeks, I felt no regret about leaving. In fact, I felt an overwhelming sense of relief, like someone making an escape, and this feeling never changed in the summers to come.

After my job was over and if the weather turned hot, my father sometimes tried to get me to come back to work for a day. He would join me at the breakfast table, open the paper, and start talking, a few angry sentences about too many drivers being on vacation, about the temperature hovering in the nineties, about people drinking like crazy. He never looked at me when he spoke, and he never addressed me directly. He appeared lost in his own thoughts, muttering to himself, but I knew what he said was meant for me. I was supposed to ask to help, not the other way around. My father found it impossible to make the request. And I believe he did so because it would have meant admitting that his own ability was limited, that he too had to rely on others. To protect himself from that knowledge, he waited for me to ask. And he may also have thought that by now I should have understood that work was not really a matter of choice. But the more he talked into his paper, the less willing I was to notice him. I ate my breakfast as if I were alone in the room. I poured myself another glass of milk, cut open another roll, and gave no sign that I was listening. Finally, my father would stop talking, his body taut with anger. He would throw down the paper, shake his head, and leave without another word.

By the time I started into my routine of summer work, my grandfather had already retired. My father was now in charge of the business, and he expanded its operations until it became necessary to find a larger location. He found one in Wandsbek, twenty minutes from our house, where there was enough room for additional trucks and two more forklifts. A month or so after the move, I stopped by the new place to drop off some papers. It was a busy day, hot, and the yard was full of motion. Before I reached the office, I spotted my father rushing toward one of the trucks. His body was bent forward, almost falling, and his legs were racing to keep up. When he reached the truck, he began shouting at the forklift driver, who was just getting ready to unload. From a distance I couldn't tell what he was saying, but I knew it had something to do with things not happening fast enough. I had seen this before. But then the moment shifted, and my father didn't calm down or walk away as he usually did. He became even more agitated, and then he leaped past the forklift and started tearing into the full pallet of beer still on the truck. His arms shot up like pistons, and the crates flew down one after another, growing into tall stacks next to the forklift. The driver looked on in silence, and so did the other men all over the yard, who stopped whatever they were doing and watched my father as if he were a ghost.

I too watched without stirring. There was no point to what my father was doing. The forklift would have finished the job in no time at all. But the pointlessness I saw then is not what I read behind my father's movements now. Once again, I notice his arms shooting up to the crates, his body spinning into a blur. I can see the frustration on his face, and I know that when he starts out he thinks about teaching a lesson to the man on the forklift. But then the man on the forklift disappears, and so do the other men watching from across the yard. Then, I disappear. And now my father is alone, and the crates keep flying into his body, faster and faster, and are flung out again, their weight welcome and longed for like a sure and steady embrace.

My brother surprised us all. In the spring of 1984, a few months before my high school graduation, he announced his decision to become part of Kirchhoff & Sons. He had finished an apprenticeship at a local wholesale company that traded in carpets and stereos, and all of us had expected him to stay on. He had never expressed an interest in the business, and my father had never asked. I wasn't there when my brother told my father about his decision, but I later learned that my father's reaction was cool and reserved. "We will see about that," he told my brother, who was stunned and hurt. But my brother didn't change his mind and started a week later. During the first year, he came close to giving up several times. He would arrive at the business around six in the morning, an hour after my father, and the day would stretch in front of him without end, an obstacle course to be run under my father's scrutiny. If the work in the office slowed down, my brother had to race out into the yard and pitch in, and when the work outside was done, it was time to rush back into the office. Each night he came home to his apartment and slipped into a hot bath, where his girlfriend would often find him sound asleep.

Now, fifteen years later, my brother is at the head of Kirchhoff & Sons. The business has moved again, from Wandsbek to Barsbüttel on the outskirts of the city, a place with enough room for eighty men and thirty trucks. I've lost count of the forklifts, but whenever I visit they buzz around me like the wasps I used to wash out of the Müllkisten. My brother's office overlooks most of the yard, making it easy for him to check the trucks' coming and going. His office is small and functional, but he has found the time to put up two framed posters. Both are cartoon prints that show the same character, a plump and contented looking duck with one wing wrapped around a cocktail. In the print behind my brother's chair, the duck rides a surfboard under the shadow of a gigantic wave. Next to the surfboard and right above the caption, two shark fins slice through the water's surface. The caption reads, "Staying Cool." The other print hangs over by the door, where the duck lies spread out on a blanket, soaking up sunshine and listening to a radio. It looks almost peaceful, except for the four crocodiles inching toward the blanket from all sides, their eyes wide open, awake, and hungry. The caption reads, "Getting away from it all."

These days, my brother no longer spends much time out in the beer yard, and even if he wanted to, he couldn't. After seven hernias, lifting anything heavier than a small case of mineral water is a problem. His wife carries the suitcases when they travel, and his son and daughter have learned not to jump into his arms. Most mornings my brother is up between three and four. He gets home around six or seven in the evening, unless it is summer and warm and people drink like crazy. Such days will keep him in his office until ten at night, waiting for the last truck to return. On Sundays, he spends the afternoon in front of his computer at home. A lot of customers now order their drinks over the weekend, and my brother listens to their messages in his house and types them into the system to get a head start on the week. I have become used to finding my brother tired when we meet. For someone who is thirty-seven, he moves with the deliberate care that belongs to an older man. His face has thinned out over the last few years, leaving his cheekbones too pronounced and his eyes too far back in their sockets. He drinks about twenty cups of coffee a day. He drinks it like a kind of fuel without which his body would refuse to give what he asks. A couple of doctors have told my brother that his heart isn't what it should be, but I don't know all the details. It is something he doesn't like to talk about.

My father retired last year. At first, he still came to the business late in the morning and stayed for a few hours. But then he stopped coming altogether. I'm not sure about his routine now. I don't know when he gets up or how he spends most of his days. I do know that on weekends he still likes to go for long bike rides. It is one interest he has managed to keep alive for some years. He will go for thirty or forty miles by himself, but he can't go as fast as he used to. His heart muscle is damaged. Over the last year, my father and my mother have begun to travel a bit, something they haven't had much time for and that might give them a chance to relearn each other's company. My mother has told me she is nervous about the hours that now belong to them together. On their last trip they went to Austria for a couple of weeks, and my father skied almost every day, while my mother took walks through the village. Two days before their return, my father ended up in a collision on the slopes. His leg and back were badly bruised, and he had to go to the hospital for x-rays. Nothing turned out to be broken, but the doctor discovered a couple of ribs that had cracked a long time ago and grown together crooked. My father tells me this on the phone from Hamburg. He remembers the injury. One of the forklift drivers hadn't seen him standing behind a pallet of beer and crushed him against a wall. "It was bad," my father says. "I could barely breathe. Should have seen a doctor, I guess." And then he chuckles as if he has told a decent joke.

In my apartment in America, I keep the phone in my study, and a call from Germany always begins with the telltale delay of a long-distance connection. It is just a brief moment, but serves as a reminder that my choices have led me away from my hometown. They have brought me to a small place in Iowa, where I study and teach writing in a landscape that sometimes reminds me of the marshes around Hamburg. The calls from Germany come at different times. My mother likes to pick up the phone in the afternoon over a cup of coffee and so catches me in the middle of the morning. But there are also calls that reach me around nine o'clock at night, and they are always from my brother.

He calls me on his car phone on his way to work. If I listen carefully, I can hear the shifting of gears in the background. On rainy days I can also pick up the soft thud of wipers and the hum of tires rolling over wet asphalt. I know my brother has his car seat tilted almost all the way back. It's the way he likes to drive, even though I have told him it's dangerous. He could slide out from under his seatbelt in an accident.

"How are you?" my brother asks.

"Oh, I'm fine," I say. "Just working on some class stuff for tomorrow. What about you?"

"The usual," he says, and I can hear the clicking of the turn signal beneath his words.

I ask about his family, his son, Felix, and his daughter, Annika. Then I ask about the business, and he gives me a rundown of meetings and men on vacation and the weather. At some point, my brother asks how my work is going. I have been waiting for that question. I always wait for it, and want my answer to come out right. I say something about the papers I'm writing and what I have my students read for class. But then I get worried that I haven't made myself clear. There is also a set of student essays to grade, I tell my brother, which will take me about twenty hours to finish. And there are the three books I have on my reading list for next week. About a thousand pages, I say. And before I realize what I'm doing, I've begun to stack hours, books, and pages like crates, one on top of the other.

Sometimes, when my brother and I talk, I remember bits and pieces from the summers I helped out at the business. The sound of the forklift or the heat inside the truck cabs. I think of my father and grandfather in those moments. But I also think of Peter, Hans's son, who, like me, left the business for good, and who never again found his bearings. Years ago, after his string of short-term jobs, he went into early retirement, filling more and more of his days with drink and tranquilizers. Since that time, stories about Peter have floated through my family like whispers. He has driven his car through the wall of his garage. He has collapsed in his apartment and out on the street, and been rushed to the hospital by ambulance. He calls my mother and yells at her in words she cannot make out. He is alone, and the vacuum through which he is falling scares me. His life isn't mine, and yet I heed it like a warning, as if moving away from the business were a way of courting certain failure.

I know it is not. I have left the business to live with work rather than through it, which is a gain. But my hold on that gain is tentative, and my father's lessons still sit in my bones and muscles. It takes little for them to pull me back into their heady promise. On some nights all it takes is my brother's voice.

"Almost there," my brother says, as he makes the final turn. I can see the corner in my mind, a sharp left next to a bus stop, which at this time of day is always empty.

"Well, I'd better let you go then," I say. "Hope the day doesn't get too crazy."

"I hope not," he says. "You go to it, all right."

"I will," I say, and what I mean is that I love him and hope what we are doing is enough.

Field Work

A turtle and a rabbit. At each end of the field I pulled the throttle toward the turtle, stepped on the brake, and turned the tractor around. Once I had realigned the wheels, I released the brake and pushed the throttle back toward the rabbit. It was an easy, almost hypnotic repetition of movements that propelled me back and forth across the seventy-acre field. With each turn I took, the glistening brown of fresh earth slowly ate its way into the dull gray of dry ground. To protect myself from the December cold, I had put on my blue wool cap and Don's old barn jacket. Two aprons hooked up alongside the tractor channeled waves of warm air toward me, the smell of oil and gasoline included. Sometimes the air in the San Joaquin Valley is clear enough to reveal the crisp outline of the Sierra Nevadas, but on this last day of 1984 the mountains stayed hidden in a white haze, making their magnitude a task for the imagination.

I had started disking in the early afternoon, right after lunch. On most days, Don and I would come back to the farmhouse at noon, have two ham sandwiches and a glass of milk, and then leave again to continue the morning's work. Ever since my arrival on the farm in late October, I had appreciated the clear-cut rhythm of the days. It wasn't just the steady pace of predictable mealtimes and work hours; it was the rhythm of the work itself. Out in the fields, plowing, disking, or shredding, I never really thought that I was working, putting in hours for a farming business whose main goal was to make a profit. Out in the fields, I felt drawn close to the ground, letting my thoughts be turned upside down as plow or disk flipped the earth on its back. Somehow, the size of the fields, each of them bordered only by more space, gave me room to daydream, to bend my story whichever way I pleased.

I was nineteen back then, fresh out of German high school, and perfectly unsure about the direction I wanted to take. I had come to California with the vague desire to plunge into something new, something that promised to slow down the respectable progression from high school to university, if only for a few months. America had seemed like the right place for such a project. Like most of my friends in Hamburg, I carried a shorthand version of the country in my head, splintered images from movies and songs that had been around for as long as I could remember — tight-lipped men on horseback; large highways vanishing into nothing but distance; tall, sleepless cities that flicker like embers at night. At nineteen, I knew the images were skewed, but I still expected America to be an adventure. And I expected California to be a distillation of America, its sun-filled essence leaning out into the Pacific Ocean.

The letter of introduction Don had sent from the farm in early September, after friends had put us in touch, didn't have much to do with any of this. Included in the letter was a picture of the farm taken from a small airplane, and all it showed was a green carpet of fields, crisscrossed by small roads running at right angles. Near the center of the picture, the words "our house" floated above a cluster of trees. A bit further to the right, at the end of a black arrow pointing nowhere, I read: "Town, five miles." Tulare, Don explained in the letter, had some twenty-five thousand people, most of them working in agriculture. His own five hundred–acre farm, where he lived with his mother, wife, and daughter, produced cotton, corn, wheat, and alfalfa. Other crops I would find in the valley were grapes, peaches, apricots, plums, almonds, pistachios, and lots of walnuts. The average annual rainfall was eight inches, most of which would fall during my visit, usually between late December and the first of March.

Don must have known that his letter would surprise me. "After reading all the above information," he wrote at the end of the three typed, single-spaced pages, "you may decide that this kind of situation is too strange for you." But the thought never crossed my mind. If Tulare wasn't the California I had expected, it would still be different from Hamburg, which in my reasoning was enough to make it attractive. Moreover, there was something about the letter I liked. I was flattered that a man more than twice my age would take the time to tell me about his town, his family, the landscape and climate he lived in day by day. Don wrote like someone who didn't worry about making the wrong impression, which, at nineteen, I secretly admired.

A month after the letter, in mid-October, I began packing — a large suitcase and a backpack. I bought a Levi's jean jacket, stone-washed, hoping it would help me look competent and distract from the fact that all I knew how to do was mow my parents' lawn. My two best friends, Bertram and Frank, gave me a large pocketknife and a picture showing me tied to a totem pole. The knife, they told me with a grin, would allow me to escape unexpected difficulties. It was a good joke, and the knife was a good one too, well balanced, the blade closing with a soft click. It took me a while to find an appropriate gift for Don, who had agreed to let me come to the farm for four months. From the letter, I knew he had done some Peace Corps work in India in the late sixties, and so I considered it a lucky break when I discovered a beer stein with a picture of the Taj Mahal.

I enjoyed running my errands for clothes and gifts. They were small tasks, easily managed, and they reminded me that I had no real commitments to worry about. Graduation was like an oversize merit badge, which made any immediate ambition unnecessary. I had tossed around the idea of law school but without serious investment. The thought of being a lawyer appealed to me in the abstract. I had visions of juggling language and logic on behalf of the poor. In the career I had mapped out for myself, I would build a reputation for fairness and dedication, and I would wear jeans even in court, shocking my older, more formal colleagues. It was one option of many. There would be time for real plans, after California, when I would come back to Hamburg and its predictable pace. For now, I was ready to fall into whatever was in front of me, sure that each decision I made could be changed and each step I took retaken.

It was Don who picked me up at the Los Angeles airport. When I walked into the lounge, he was leaning against one of the pillars with his arms crossed in front of him. He wore a light-brown leather vest, plaid shirt, jeans, and a pair of cowboy boots. His face had a deep tan, turning red across the cheekbones, framed by short gray hair that looked freshly cut. A small black pipe sat in the left corner of his mouth, the sign we had agreed on. "Mr. Brown?" I asked, worried I could be talking to a stranger. He pushed himself away from the pillar and put out his hand. "Welcome." It was an uneven handshake, his hand swallowing mine with a thud of callus and muscle. "Did you have a good flight?" I nodded, still confused by the nine hours that had dropped into my lap somewhere above the Atlantic. We picked up my luggage and made our way to the car. The heat outside the airport and the taxis and shuttles darting off to their unknown destinations punctured my exhaustion. For the first time, I realized how far I had traveled. There was a sudden, worried rush in my stomach, and all I could think of was to keep my eyes on Don's back.

After we left the parking area, Don hit Interstate 405, taking us north to San Fernando. I tried to keep my head in the cool breeze of the air conditioner and watched the cars flying past us. For a few minutes I counted convertibles, and the numbers added up faster than I had thought possible. Less than a day ago, in Hamburg, October had meant blustery days and a sense of slowing down for winter. Now, everything moved with the urgency of spring. At the bottom of the Santa Susanna Mountains the traffic thinned out, and we began to climb Highway 5 toward Tejon Pass. Don asked about my family, and I tried to answer as best as I could. My English wasn't bad, but it still carried the touch of classroom exercises and vocabulary lists. "Yes, all of us live in Hamburg." "My brother is four years older than I am." Seven convertibles in ten minutes. We crossed the pass. "Just a few more miles and you'll be able to see the valley," Don said, making me strain my neck to get a better view.

It was an unexpected vista. The hills that had lined the highway for the past forty miles or so suddenly broke away on both sides, leaving a gaping hole of sky and distance. The valley floor stretched out in front of us: brown, green, and yellow squares dancing along the thin line of highway, spinning off to the left and right under the scattered shadows of clouds. I remembered the bird's-eye picture Don had sent me in his letter. The plane from which the picture had been taken must have traveled at just about the same height from which we now slowly descended into the valley.

When I stepped out of the farmhouse on my first day of work, my legs felt soft and jittery. One of Don's two collies came barking up the stairs the moment she saw me and started sniffing my new boots. I wore my Levi's jacket and a pair of jeans. The knife sat in my back pocket, adding some reassuring weight. Don had told me that I would arrive during cotton harvest, but I had no idea yet what that meant or how I would figure into it. He had left the house a few minutes before me, and I could see him and Scott, his full-time help, working next to the barn, getting the two cotton pickers ready for the day. Even from a distance the machines looked huge, their front wheels as tall as the men. Don and Scott worked quickly, each movement grown smooth from practice.

"Morning," Don said, as he saw me coming toward him.

"Good morning," I answered. "What are you doing?"

"Greasing the picking heads; there are plenty of things spinning around in here." Don patted the machine and pointed to two slots that opened at the front of the picker.

"See those spindles? There are more than a thousand, each one spinning around its own axis and also going around in circles with the entire cylinder. The spindles are what rips the cotton out of the boll."

I glanced at the one bar of spindles that was visible from my angle. Each spindle was about four inches long and had been polished to a sparkling silver from recent use. They looked like a set of impressive teeth, sharp and precise, ready to devour whatever happened to stand in their path.

"We'll have you running one of the pickers in a few days," Don said and handed me a grease gun. I wasn't sure whether to feel flattered or scared. But the grease gun, at least, was easy to handle, and I was glad to have something to do.

For two days I rode along on Don's picker. There was a small platform outside the driver's cabin that had enough room for a second person to stand. On the first day, I stayed out on the platform and watched Don, trying to memorize the movements of his arms and legs. The noise of the engine and picking heads was loud enough to force us to shout whenever I had a question or Don wanted to explain something. But for long stretches of time there was no need to talk, and I had a chance to look out over the white field, which the midday sun lit up like snow. In the bright light I had to squint my eyes to see Scott working alongside us, gliding through the cotton at the same slow pace. Each pass the pickers took cut dark lines across the field where the cotton had been pulled out of the bolls. To me, who had never seen this kind of harvest, it looked like drawing: two hands moving across a seventy-acre canvas, working in charcoal.

After every two rounds the picker would be full, and Don drove up to one of the trailers parked at the edge of the field. There, he pulled back the lever next to his seat, and the basket behind us would start tilting sideways, open up, and release the cotton in a quiet avalanche. At the end of our third unloading, Don shut off the engine and told me to jump into the trailer. "Jump in?" I asked. "You want me to jump into the cotton?" He laughed, his face in the shadow of a red seed cap. "Sure, go right ahead." But before I could move, he had already jumped himself and disappeared up to his thighs. I jumped in after him and sank down to my waist. "You see," Don said, still laughing at the look on my face, "we tramp the cotton to get as much into the trailer as possible. Nobody wants to take more trips to the gin than necessary." He held on to the side of the trailer and began walking. I followed him. It felt like treading water, like climbing stairs that continuously gave way, like slipping into a dream in which all was slow motion. The heat seemed to double, and my shirt began to stick to my back. Sweat ran into my eyes and sent my glasses sliding down my nose. I thought of Bertram and Frank, and how much I wanted them to see me right now, tramping cotton in California, the same stuff our mothers used to wipe off their makeup at night. And the more I watched myself through the eyes of my friends, the more consciously I moved, trying to look casual, tramping cotton as if I had been doing it all my life.

At lunchtime, Don's wife, Janet, came out to the field to bring us some food and pick up the next trailer for the gin. She was a slender, soft-spoken woman who struck me as shy during those first days. For the past two mornings, I had seen her only briefly, a blinding headache making her grope for painkillers in one of the kitchen cabinets before she slipped back into the dark bedroom. Even now she was wearing sunglasses to protect her eyes and keep the next migraine at bay. After a few weeks, I would learn that she often sat up late at night at the living room table to have a cigarette and cup of coffee, lights out and the TV murmuring in the background. Don would already be asleep on the couch by then, but I sometimes joined her. We never talked much, maybe just a few offhand comments about one of the shows or something that had happened during the day. She always listened carefully to what I said, but she didn't seem much interested in giving direction to our talk. Inside the blue flicker of the TV and the smoke from her cigarette, she kept to herself.

When Janet had pulled away with the trailer, Don and I continued our rounds as before. We worked until it got too dark to see where we had already picked. The next day, Don let me take over the steering wheel, shouting directions over my shoulder and guiding my hands when necessary. Then, after a few more hours of team picking, I was on my own. I sat on the edge of the driver's seat, hands wrapped around the steering wheel, eyes glued to the two rows of cotton vanishing into the picker. Don's advice ran through my head like ticker tape. Slow down a few yards before you get to the end of the field. Lift the picking heads to have enough clearance for the turn. Get the picker close enough to the trailer before you unload. I drove round after round, and eventually I relaxed. Don watched me for a little while and then found something else to do. His confidence in my ability surprised me. If he was worried about letting me drive the picker, whose loss would have doubled the length of the harvest, he didn't let it show.

When nothing out of the ordinary had happened at the end of the first week, Don started up a one-row picker he hadn't used in years. It was really an old tractor that had been converted into a picker, and it looked like it would fall apart any minute. There was no driver's cabin, just a metal seat sticking into the air. Its large steering wheel had half a revolution of play, which made it almost impossible to drive a straight line. But Don managed to get the picker to the field even though his arms had to stay busy all the time, steering left, then right, just to keep the picker under control. He looked funny, like a child driving an imaginary school bus, and it didn't take Don long to notice that Scott and I had a good time watching him. When we passed each other again in the field, he stood up from his seat, put on his cap backward, clenched the pipe between his teeth, and, eyes wide open, spun the steering wheel like a sailor caught in a storm. Scott and I howled; it was a ridiculous sight. He thought up several more postures during the afternoon, at one time acting like a mad general in front of his army, at another puffing his pipe and scanning the land with the inflated passion of an art critic.

We finished the field at dusk and drove back to the farmhouse single file. Jenni, Don's fourteen-year-old daughter, met us halfway on her Honda three-wheeler. She spent most of her time after school riding her cycle, and she had become a good, reckless driver. With her headlights on, she wove tight circles around the three pickers, dancing between us like a firefly. I watched her escapades and had to laugh. I was relieved to have made it through the first week without major disasters. I was relieved to learn that the place I had spent months imagining seemed to have a niche for me. Whenever possible, I had watched Don and Scott to pick up some of their sureness, trying not to seem hesitant or scared. And I had sought out any dirt I could find to get the newness out of my clothes. In the dim light of the driver's cabin, I checked my boots for the first signs of wear.

Don's mother, Eugenia, lived about half a mile north of the farmhouse. She was in her early seventies, a retired grade-school teacher who still spoke with the mild cadence aimed at unruly classrooms. She lived by herself, and when she wasn't helping out at church or taking care of her vegetable garden, she spent most days in her kitchen. In the afternoons, she liked to sit at her kitchen table and write letters to friends. For a number of years she had hosted students from abroad, and a good many of her letters, even after two or three decades, still traveled to Greece, Germany, Denmark, and Finland. She had picked up a few German words along the way, and she enjoyed trying them out on me, pronouncing them with a soft blur that made them sound foreign.

When we started picking the cotton east of her house, she came out to the field several times and invited us in for some lemonade. She was easy to talk to, full of intense curiosity. Everything seemed worth her attention — a red-tailed hawk hunting outside her window, a thunderstorm moving along the foothills, a newspaper story about the true density of black holes. She wanted to know what happened around her, and she didn't mind asking questions. I liked listening to her and answering her string of questions because I too felt that most of what I saw during those first days required a second look. The farm was becoming a real place, but it was also still strange and could splinter into puzzles. There were the hummingbirds whose buzz, when I heard it for the first time, slipped me back into a fairy tale about fist-sized bees. There was the stillborn calf we pulled out of its mother with a come-along, its body so limp and slender that it made me think of an eel. And there was the cotton, light and insubstantial, falling like snow into the basket behind me.

The new field we had moved to was smaller than the last one, and Scott and I could drive four rounds before having to unload the pickers. I was getting used to the pace of the work and stopped playing in my head the motion of pedals, levers, and steering wheel. Things began to feel natural, and that was when I made my mistake. After another trip to the trailer, I eased the picker back into the field. Everything seemed fine for the first twenty yards or so, the two rows of cotton disappearing at an even pace under my seat. Then, I noticed a slight change in engine pitch. A second later, the picker lurched like a train jumping its tracks, almost shaking me out of the seat. I shut down the engine as fast as I could and climbed out of the cabin. Behind the picker lay thirty yards of destruction, a tornado alley of mangled cotton. Only a handful of plants were still standing, the rest had either been brushed to the ground or jammed into the picking heads, which I had forgotten to engage. I knelt down in front of the picker and tried to loosen the solid mass of branches and cotton, but no matter how hard I pulled or pushed, nothing moved.

By the time Don showed up, I felt nauseous. "Looks like you've had a bit of a problem," he said, poking at the jam with his boot. I was too embarrassed to say anything. Whatever story I had put together in my head, starring myself in the role of sunburned field hand, had been mangled along with the cotton. And the longer Don stared at the mess I had made, the more I felt found out, a city boy with two left hands and a short memory. "Well," Don finally said, "we'd better back the picker out of here and see what we can do." He didn't sound mad. With the help of a hammer, a crowbar, and a knife, it took him half an hour to clean out the heads, and when he was done, he sent me back into the field.

We stopped picking earlier than usual that day. Don was the president of the local 4-H club, and this was the night he and Janet were hosting the annual Halloween party. About half an hour before sundown the first cars started pulling into the driveway, and soon the place was filled with people. The parents and older children stood chatting in small groups, while the younger kids ran up and down the driveway. Some of them climbed onto the tractors, others kicked up dust and turned their flashlights into laser swords. The night's attraction was going to be a hayride, and when it was dark enough, Don told us to get up onto the large flatbed trailer, which he had loaded with bales earlier in the day. He hooked up the trailer to one of the tractors and pulled out into the road. It was a clear night. The lights of other farms stretched along the horizon, flickering in the heat coming off the ground.

The ride took less than fifteen minutes. I knew we were going to a patch of woods behind Eugenia's house, not far from a small creek, where everything was ready for a bonfire and s'mores. Janet had explained s'mores to me the night before, and I wasn't sure yet whether I wanted to try one. Marshmallows, chocolate, and crackers, all at once, sounded like too much of a good thing. After we reached the woods, Don lit the fire while the rest of us pulled bales off the trailer and arranged them in a circle. The fire grew quickly, and the nearby oak trees began to move out of the shadows. In the flickering light their leaves arched above us like a tremendous roof.

Someone had brought along copies of campfire songs, and for a while we sang about ghosts and vampires, our voices sounding slim and muffled under the trees. After the singing, one of the younger boys put himself in charge of teaching me how to build my s'more. He was dressed in a wizard's cape and delivered his instructions slowly and earnestly. When he was pleased with what he saw, he told me where to place my bundle in the fire. The s'more was good, much better than I had expected, and I put together a second one as soon as I had finished the first. All of us were busy eating now, and when most of the noise had died away, Don got up from his seat, moved next to the fire, and began to look around the circle of faces. "You know," he said with a hint of reluctance in his voice, "I wasn't sure whether to have our bonfire in this place, on this night of the year." Some of the adults started smiling, but there was complete silence now, except for the sound of the fire.

It was a good story, and Don told it as if it could be true. Sometimes his words slowed down to a trickle, only to speed up again the next moment, slipping us into the arms and legs of a man running from an apparition. That night, I found it easy to believe in ghosts, and when Don pointed to a stretch of road not far from where we sat, I looked hard, expecting something to come out of the darkness. Halloween and the bonfire had loosened my imagination. But it was also the sound of the words that pulled me into the story, the cadence of a still-foreign language that could turn the ordinary into mystery. And, of course, there was the memory of my accident in the field, a reminder that this new place could fall out from under me without warning. I was cut off from the things I knew well, and that made the supernatural seem plausible. On our way back to the house, the trailer bouncing along the curves of the creek, I kept looking over to the road, turning each headlight into a floating lantern.

It took us two more weeks to finish the first round of picking. I had been surprised when Don told me we would return to every field a second time, but now, as we got ready to do so, the reason was obvious. Apart from the cotton we had missed, many of the late bolls had needed extra time to dry up and explode into tiny white clouds. The main difference during second picking was that we didn't have to unload nearly as often as before. We could pick for two hours without making a trip to the trailer, which was both convenient and dangerous. Two hours of steady engine noise and nothing to look at but cotton and distance could empty one's mind, and from there it was just a small step into sleep. Scott dozed off on the third day. I saw his picker make a sharp turn to the left and rip diagonally through the field, bucking like a horse. After a few seconds the picker stopped and Scott climbed out of the cabin. He looked over at me, waved, and then began to stretch and yawn. We joked about his nap for several days, and maybe I brought up the story more often than I should have. I didn't mind that my own accident was no longer the only one.

As the nights got cooler during the second half of November, we often had to wait for the morning sun to burn off the dew before we could start picking. If the cotton was too wet, it stuck to our spindles like gum. Sometimes fog kept us out of the field for a whole day. This wasn't the kind of fog I knew from home, a thin gauze that gave halos to street lamps. Tulare fog, as Don called it, was thick and slow, a wall of white that forced you to re-create the world from memory. Schools closed down, cars crawled along roads, and even sound seemed sluggish. After one such fog, the local paper printed a satellite picture of California, and only the Central Valley showed up perfectly white, like an eye without an iris. I cut out the picture and pinned it to my bedroom wall. The thought that I had been underneath that whiteness, alone, breathing and thinking, thrilled me. Somehow it felt like an accomplishment.

On the days when we couldn't pick, Don usually had a number of smaller projects lined up. For a while, we cut wood from an old oak tree that had tipped over in one of the fields. Don showed me how to use an ax and how to read the grain of the wood to get the least resistance. I struggled with the ax at first, my blade dancing all over the chopping block, but then I fell into my own rhythm — the slow set-up, the final aim, the swift release of muscle and metal. The other projects we had waiting on wet days were mostly repair jobs. Some piece of machinery or equipment always needed Don's attention, and since I knew nothing about mechanics, I spent those days looking over his shoulder. Occasionally I helped out by holding a bolt or tightening a couple of screws, but that was all. I didn't mind watching Don though. He walked back and forth between his tools and his machines, fixing each problem at a steady pace and explaining to me what he was doing. I usually picked up a couple of new words during the repairs, words that felt like they had their own gravity. *Head gasket. Carburetor. Camshaft. Transmission fluid.* I tried to pronounce the words just right, slow and broad, and each time I succeeded I caught a glimpse of my other self — the nineteen-year-old who had grown up in the valley, who had taken apart more engines than he cared to remember.

For some of the repairs, Don had to get parts in town, and I went along as often as possible. I liked riding in his pickup truck, an old GMC Sierra permanently loaded with everything from chains and crowbars to shovels and irrigation pipes. The truck's cab was as cluttered as the back. Screwdrivers, wrenches, cardboard boxes, and old receipts piled up on the dashboard, and all of it was covered by a fine brown dust that reminded me of powdered sugar. I could never tell what to expect on these trips to town. Don was ready to interrupt our drive whenever he saw something along the road I should know about. Once we stopped next to a walnut orchard so I could watch the work of the harvesting machines, how they grabbed the trees and then shook off the nuts into aprons that looked like giant bat-wings. Another time, Don spotted a spray helicopter parked in a nearby field. He turned off the road and arranged a ride for me. A minute later I was airborne, suspended above the valley in a slow swinging pendulum. I tried to keep my bearings, but I didn't manage for very long. The helicopter swung back and forth, sky and fields turned liquid, and the difference between up and down disappeared.

Don made an effort to show me as much about the valley as possible. And I could tell he didn't mind doing so. At times, he seemed as intrigued by what he showed me as I was. He was able to listen to his own words with an air of curiosity, as if he was still surprised that the things around him existed in the first place. In his left shirt pocket he carried a small circular slide rule that he would pull out on occasion to work on some idea that had just occurred to him. Sometimes he calculated fertilizer concentrations or the number of seed bags he would need, but more often he used it just to play around, to find out how many gallons of creek water rushed past us in one minute, or how long a field he would own if he planted all of his cotton in one row. I loved watching him work the slide rule, his fingers dancing around the thin plastic disk, his head cocked sideways. For a moment he would forget all about the day's projects and lose himself in a question that needed no answer. Even though he had lived on the farm for most of his life, and as far as I could tell knew it better than anyone, he seemed in no danger of exhausting the place or growing numb to what it offered.

With the interruptions caused by rain and fog, second picking kept us busy until the end of November. On the last day we were all eager to be done, and Don once more started up the old one-row picker to move things along. With the end of the harvest in sight, we grew more reluctant to interrupt the picking at all, and we delayed our trips to the trailer as long as possible. Sometimes that meant we had to stop in the middle of the field, climb up into the basket, and tramp the cotton to make more room. By the time I finished the last round, my picker was more than ready to be unloaded. But as I drove out of the field, my back wheel got stuck in some wet, muddy ground. No matter how carefully I played with clutch and throttle, I couldn't move forward. Finally, I shifted into reverse, and my back wheel broke without warning. It made a spectacular sound, like an amplified gunshot that refused to go away. The picker crashed backward and sent me tumbling through the driver's cabin. When I looked up again, all I could see was sky.

Don and Scott had a hard time calming me down. I was convinced that I had ruined the machine, which now sat at the edge of the field like a heap of prehistoric bones. "Don't worry about it," Don said, "these things happen." But I could tell by the way he scrutinized the damage that his mind wasn't at ease. He circled the picker a couple of times and decided we should go back to the house for now. There was nothing we could do without tools. Three days later, Don would find a spare back wheel at a junkyard for seventy dollars and get the picker to run again without too much trouble. On the day of the accident, however, I had no idea things would turn out that way, and when we reached the house I was too shaken up to do any other work. I went inside, grabbed a towel, and slipped into the shower. The hot water felt good, but my mind wouldn't let go of what had happened. I was upset, and I became more upset when I realized how badly I wanted to be in my room in Hamburg next to my parents and brother, where nothing like this could happen. I turned off the shower and got dressed. For the rest of the afternoon, I lay on the floor in the living room and stared at the television.

Don came in a couple of hours later. "Guess what?" he said, falling into the chair next to me. "I just spoke with Charley Fisher. Same thing happened to one of his men today. Snapped the back wheel clear off."

It took me a second to understand what I had just heard.

"You mean he did the same thing?"

"Yes, got it caught in some soft ground just like you did. Happens pretty easily, really. Well, I had better get out of these clothes and take my shower too." Don got up and disappeared into the bathroom. I was convinced I had dreamed up our exchange. Someone else had broken off the back wheel of his picker. I took a deep breath and walked over to the window. The two collies were chasing each other up and down the driveway. I watched them for a while, shifting my weight from one leg to the other, already forgetting the room in Hamburg I had longed for a moment ago.

I was glad that the next round of work looked easy. Now that the cotton was gone, the three-foot-high plants had to be shredded and their roots cut. Shredding wasn't much harder than driving a car. All I had to do was keep the tractor moving while the shredder cut four rows down to stubble. There was nothing to worry about during the turns, no hairpin maneuvers on three wheels, no lifting and lowering of picking heads. I liked how the shredding changed the look of the fields, lowering them back to the ground until the harvest seemed to belong to a distant season. It was the first time since my arrival that I recognized fall, the familiar feeling of a year winding down, despite the sunshine and the lush eucalyptus trees. I often scared up pheasants on my rounds with the shredder, making them scramble for cover in a field growing smaller by the minute. When I reached the last four rows, I made it a game to spot the birds I knew were in front of me, but I never could. They blended in too perfectly and each time startled me with their sudden escapes. Twice I saw a coyote sitting at the edge of the field, watching the pheasants scramble with a bored expression before he turned away and vanished.

The tractor Don let me use had a radio built into the cab, and after trying out different stations, I kept it tuned to Y-94 FM. It was a classic-hit station and played several songs I knew. Since I was sure no one could hear me inside the cab and over the roar of the shredder, I got into the habit of singing along with the songs, tapping out their beat on the steering wheel. Sometimes I sang at the top of my lungs, imitating the voices I heard no matter how high or low they climbed. I thought I sounded pretty good. Together with the minimal attention the job required, the music sent my mind drifting in all directions. Late in the afternoons, when the sun sat low in the sky and I began to feel tired, all the songs sounded like movie themes, providing background for the stories stacking up inside my head.

One of the faces I thought of on those afternoons belonged to Julia Fernandes, a girl I had met a couple of weeks earlier at one of Jenni's basketball games. Like Jenni, she played for the varsity team, and I had been introduced to her a few minutes before the game. She had smiled at me that night and had asked how I liked Tulare, and then, while I was still working on my answer, had been called away by the coach for the warm-up routine. I ended up seeing little of the game because I mostly watched her. She looked older than Jenni, maybe seventeen or eighteen, had shoulder-length brown hair, and was taller than anyone else on the court. Her height slowed her down just enough to make her arms and legs move with a kind of graceful imprecision that reminded me of a dancer. When the game was over I hoped for another chance to talk, but in the midst of everyone leaving the gym I couldn't find her.

A couple of days after the game, Don pointed out her house to me on one of our trips to town. It was a red two-story structure with a wide lawn, and I tried to imagine what it looked like on the inside. I had no way of knowing whether Julia Fernandes had given a second thought to our meeting. In fact, I thought it likely she had forgotten about it. But somehow that realization didn't keep me from thinking up future encounters between us, elaborate scenarios in which we slowly drifted toward each other, helpless in the face of our mutual attraction. I patched together stories that would have made me groan if I had come across them in a novel. And yet each one of them held my complete attention. The scene I had worked out most clearly was the first visit to her house, where her family would be waiting in a large, tasteful living room, eager to meet me. Apart from the parents, there would be several brothers and sisters, all of them tall and dark, who would shake my hand and wonder what kind of man I was. Afterward, during dinner, I would give straightforward answers to their questions. I would sound self-assured but not arrogant, revealing the solid core of my character. Julia wouldn't say much throughout the meal, but I would see her smile and know that she was pleased. After a day of shredding and listening to Y-94 FM, I had no doubt that I would win over the Fernandes clan.

I kept moving ahead with the shredder, and Scott followed with the root-cutter. His was the more difficult job of the two, and I was content to leave it to him. Don kept busy with repairs next to the barn. Lucy, one of Jenni's two pigs, was ready to have her litter, and Don didn't want to be too far away when the time came. He had already put her in the farrowing crate, where she had settled down with an air of timeless patience. Normally, Lucy had a fickle temper. When I had fed her before, I had flung the corn into her trough from a safe distance. I didn't trust her. I thought there was cunning behind her watery, blue eyes. Don and Scott both told stories about getting chased by Lucy on her bad days, stories about last-minute escapes out of the pen. Sometimes I entered the barn and could see Lucy standing still, looking in my direction as if she had been waiting for me. I knew that was impossible, but I imagined her eyes on my back as I moved around the barn doing my chores.

Don kept checking on Lucy and finally decided it was time to stay with her. We grabbed a couple of blankets after dinner, made some coffee, and sat down in two camping chairs next to the farrowing crate. Jenni joined us for the first half hour or so. She was excited about the prospect of owning a brand-new litter and had several theories why this one should be especially large. "You can tell by the way Lucy's breathing, Dad, can't you see? And there's that look in her eyes. I'm sure we'll get at least eighteen." Don didn't argue with her, and I too nodded as if I knew what she was talking about. Jenni had strong opinions that changed almost daily. It was hard to keep up with her. When she had returned to the house, Don and I sat quietly for a while and drank our coffee. By now the cool air of the evening had found its way into the barn, and I picked up a blanket and put it over my shoulders. Through one of the windows I could hear the generator of a nearby dairy kicking in with a soft metallic hum, a sound that after almost two months had begun to feel familiar.

The first of the litter arrived shortly after eleven. Don took the towel he had brought along and began to clean the small body with careful strokes. He rubbed the snout to make sure nothing obstructed the breathing. Then he slipped the animal under a spotlight he had attached to the crate, letting its warmth ease the shock. After another couple of minutes, he lifted the piglet again and put it alongside Lucy, where it began to feed with eyes still closed. From then on the litter grew in short intervals, and Don went through the same motions with each arrival until he decided it was my turn to take over. I tried to handle the next small body with the same confidence, but I felt nervous and clumsy. "You can't hurt them with a towel," Don said. "They're stronger than you think." And to prove his point he took my hand and placed it on the back of one of the newborns at Lucy's side. I could feel the shoulder muscles slide back and forth under the soft skin. I felt the rib cage expand and contract, and underneath it I felt a restless, whirling heartbeat. I was reluctant to let go again.

Around three in the morning Lucy's litter had grown to ten, and it didn't look like she would be done anytime soon. Don told me I could turn in if I felt tired. I fought the idea of a warm bed for a few minutes, not wanting to look like a quitter, but then surrendered. Don stayed out in the barn until seven, when he came over to the house for breakfast and announced the final count of fourteen. It wasn't quite as high as Jenni had predicted, but she didn't mind. Instead, she started describing to us how she would spend the money from the sale of the litter. Her plan was to get a new helmet and racing goggles for her three-wheeler. She had already picked them out at the Honda shop in town and rattled off their features like a salesclerk.

When Scott showed up for work at eight, Don had us start up the tractors to continue with the shredding and the root-cutting. I thought that my lack of sleep would catch up with me out in the field. As a precaution, I turned up the radio and listened to Y-94 FM at twice the normal volume. The trick worked, even though I found the commercials excruciating by midafternoon. At the end of the day, I had finished most of the shredding, and Don thought I had about two hours of work left. We spent the evening trying to finish a jigsaw puzzle that we had worked on for a couple of weeks. It was something Don enjoyed doing and which I had begun to like myself. Usually we fell into slow, meandering talks while we puzzled, talks full of sudden silences as one of us picked up a piece and tried to make it fit. That night we didn't talk at all. We coasted inside our drowsiness and let our minds go blank.

It was Don's German shepherd, Ben, who pulled us back from the brink of sleep. He slipped in through the front door and made a dash for the living room table. Something had scared him. Don tried to coax Ben back outside, but he couldn't get him to move. "Someone must be using a gun out there," he said. Years ago Ben had dragged himself into Don's driveway, shot up and bleeding. Don had taken Ben to the vet, spent three hundred dollars on an operation, and kept him on the farm. The only two reminders of his injuries, I had learned, were a limp in his left front leg and a deep fear of guns. I hadn't seen Ben this afraid before, and it surprised me to see his large body curled up under the table. He looked like a different animal.

Don stepped outside and listened. I followed him, and after about a minute we heard a gunshot floating toward us from the other side of the creek. "Probably some guys hunting pheasants," Don said. "I'd better take a look." He didn't bother to put on boots but walked over to the truck in his slippers. "Do you want to come along?" I ran after him, wearing the same kind of slippers he did, an old pair he had given me for use around the house. Don disliked hunters. He saw no point in their passion, and the thought of having them on his own land made him angry. He had told me so several times on our way to town when we had seen hunters combing through neighboring fields. It was one of the things he found impossible to tolerate. He pulled out of the driveway and sped in the direction of the last shot.

The three men were in the field I had shredded earlier in the day. They had spread out across its width, walking toward the last patch of cotton. Each of them carried a shotgun. Don stopped the truck at the edge of the field, and we climbed out of the cab. It felt funny to walk across the stubble in slippers. The slippers were too big for my feet, and I had to curl up my toes to keep them from falling off. By now, the hunters had noticed our arrival and stood huddled together, waiting for us to come closer. I wished I had taken the time to put on my boots before we left. The thought of confronting these men in slippers didn't help the tightness in my stomach. What if this didn't turn out to be a friendly chat? What if these men had been drinking? In the short while it took us to cross the field, I sketched out a string of possible disasters. I wasn't used to guns. For me, guns belonged to the movies I had seen with my friends in Hamburg, something to marvel at from a safe distance.

Don was the first to speak as we reached the hunters. He sounded calm. His voice was the one I knew from our conversations.

"Good evening, gentlemen."

"Good evening." The man who answered wore hunting fatigues and a bright orange vest. Like his companions, he now held the shotgun at his side with one hand, its barrel pointing at the ground.

"I was just wondering who gave you permission to hunt on this property?" Don asked.

"Oh, the owner did. We always check beforehand."

"Well, that's funny. Because I own this field, and I don't remember anyone asking me." In the silence that followed, the man uneasily stepped from one foot to the other, looked at Don, looked at me, then back at Don. The other two men found something to stare at beyond the cotton patch.

"All I know is that we asked a guy in a pickup truck who came by, and he told us it was okay to hunt here," the man finally said.

"I don't know who that person was," Don said, "but I am now asking you to leave. I do not want any hunting on this land."

"All right then, we'll leave." The man turned around to the other two. "Let's go." They swung their shotguns back up in front of them and began to march off to the east. Don and I turned back to the truck.

We didn't drive off right away but sat in the cab for a while, watching the three men cut across to a neighboring field and then on to the highway. Now that I no longer had a reason to be afraid, I could feel my tiredness return, and I settled back into the seat with my eyes half closed. I remembered the night Don and I had spent in the barn. I recalled the play of muscles and breathing I had felt against the palm of my hand. And I thought of the hunter who had looked at me for a brief moment out in the field. I wondered what had gone through his head. Did he believe that I belonged to this place, knew it like someone who had grown up here? What else could he think? It pleased me that this was the way he might remember me — as someone connected to this land, who carried inside him the memory of its seasons, who could read its deepest map.

Don's prediction was right. It took only two more hours to finish shredding the last bit of cotton. When I was done, he put me on another tractor and had me start into the disking, the last cycle of work. And it was the disking that finally brought me out to the field on that last day of 1984, wearing my blue wool cap and Don's old barn jacket. I drove round after round that day, the disk gradually turning the field into a rich brown. A handful of birds had begun to pay attention to what I was doing. They were a beautiful bunch, all white and slender, not unlike miniature cranes with bright yellow beaks. Their system of following the tractor was unusually elaborate. Instead of staying behind the disk with short flights, they circled the entire tractor each time they wanted to get onto the freshest ground. On their way back to the disk they would come directly at the tractor, swerving only at the last moment, and then glide into place to continue their meal. I glanced at my watch. A quarter to three. It would take one more hour to finish the field. Plenty of time to get done in daylight. A quarter to three. Almost by reflex I added the nine hours to get the time in Hamburg. A quarter to three. A quarter to twelve. At home, the new year would begin in fifteen minutes.

I don't know why I had completely forgotten about it. Don, Scott, and I had started this morning like any other, getting the equipment ready, dividing up the tasks for the day. I knew, of course, that this was the last day of the year, but up until this moment I had felt no need to leave its rhythm, to worry about a second timeline along which my family and friends were traveling. Now, I remembered, and I tried to imagine what was happening in my part of the city. Even a week earlier, at Christmas, I hadn't felt this pull, this desire to put myself back among what was closest to me. I had spoken with my parents and my brother, and, as in all our other phone conversations, I had drowned them in stories about the farm and the harvest. I had hardly listened to what they told me, because it all seemed too familiar, part of what belonged to me anyway. But now, with the new year so close, I didn't feel the same indifference and I tried to get the picture right:

All day long my mother has rushed through the house. The living room looks spotless. There is a fresh bouquet of pink tulips on the dining table, and a handful of streamers are curled around the desk lamp. The meat for the fondue sits in the fridge, a mountain of lean, red squares. Next to the meat, a tray full of Berliner mit Zuckerguß, and next to the Berliner four bottles of Perrier-Jouët. My mother ordered the meat and Berliner weeks ago, but she waited till this morning to pick them up, riding the bicycle along her shopping route, getting the freshest Berliner and meat anyone could want. Whenever my mother has guests, she aspires to perfection. My father has no part in all of this. He spends the morning at work and returns home just in time to see my mother stick a little wire chimney sweep between the tulips. Around six o'clock my brother slips out of the house to party with his friends.

Much later, after my parents' guests have arrived and a few bottles of champagne have disappeared, stories begin to circle the dining table and chuckles grow into full-blown laughter. Maybe one of the guests has brought a set of lead pellets, an old custom on New Year's Eve. My mother gets out some old spoons, a few candles, and two or three glasses of cold water. Then everyone puts a piece of lead on a spoon and begins to melt it above one of the flames. As soon as the lead has become liquid, it gets dropped into the water, turning solid with an exasperated hiss. Fingers dive into glasses and snatch the still warm metal out of the water. What does it look like? A tree? An elephant? A pair of shaking hands? Nobody knows for sure what it means, but everyone has an opinion, hoping it bodes well for what lies ahead. For the past hour or so, the TV has been on, and now attention shifts to the small clock in the upper right-hand corner of the screen. The champagne glasses are filled one more time, the clock continues its steady crawl, and the party begins to wind down, slipping into the eye of the storm where everything is quiet.

For me, New Year's had always ranked on one level with Christmas. On December 27 or 28, when the novelty of gifts and visitors was wearing off, New Year's was still all promise. Soon the stores would start selling firecrackers, entire arsenals arranged under glass counters.

According to the law, we had to be at least eighteen to buy any of the colorful packages. However, the drugstore on our block, run by Frau Deunert, had a neighborly attitude in this matter. Frau Deunert knew most of the families, and she would sell firecrackers to us if we brought written permission from a parent. My mother would surrender within a day, and with the note in my pocket I wasted no time getting to the store. Frau Deunert would read the note, shoot a quick glance at me, then nod. "What would you like?" The choices seemed endless. Wunderkerzen, Böller, Bienenkörbe, Kanonenschläge, Frösche, Goldregen. What kept my purchases under control wasn't modesty or reason. The only two things that reined me in were the small amount of money I had and the fact that Frau Deunert knew my mother. The news of any oversize purchases would have reached her in five minutes.

After the trip to the store, I would spend an hour or so arranging my firecrackers in a shoe box; as soon as one pattern emerged, everything lined up according to color and size, another pattern began to look more promising, and I would start all over. But the real temptation was to go out and set off the firecrackers before it was legal to do so. Firecrackers were to be used only on New Year's Eve after six o'clock, but my friend Jens-Peter and I never followed that rule. With our coat pockets full of Böller and a couple of Bic lighters, we would sit in the back of Jens-Peter's garden and try to think up ways of using our firepower. Sometimes we would bury the Böller and blast a series of craters into the soft ground. At other times, we put the Böller under an empty tin can and sent it some forty feet into the air. The only drawback of these games was that they were hard to keep secret. Whoever wanted to find us only had to listen and look for a tin can floating above the trees.

At one minute to three I kept my eyes on the watch, trusting that I could keep the tractor more or less straight with an occasional glance ahead. The second hand wandered down the dial, passed the halfway point, and then began its climb toward the full hour. Three o'clock. Twelve o'clock. My hometown exploded. Rockets lit up the sky. The sound of church bells mingled with the bark of firecrackers. People cheered, hugged each other, champagne glasses ringing in unison. The tractor stayed perfectly straight, the engine noise a steady hum, and beneath it the sound of ground brushing against the disk blades. Some of the birds were still around, flying slow circles in search of food.

Other things happened at that moment. I lifted my feet and said to myself: "Frohes Neues Jahr." There is a ritual in my family of literally jumping into the new year. In my head I carry the image of my mother trying to keep her balance on our soft living room couch, giggling, a drink in her hand, the rules of social etiquette no longer important. She looks beautiful with her disheveled hair and flushed face, her knees bending, ready for the leap into another year. There wasn't enough room for a jump on the tractor. So instead, I lifted my feet and put them down again, hoping to attract some good luck that way.

For a split second, with my feet in the air, I was in two places at once — a calm seventy-acre field in California and a raucous city of two million in Germany. And in that brief moment, the idea of time took on a physical shape in my imagination. I thought of a giant, slow-rolling thunderstorm that moved toward me from east to west. Only the thunder had nothing to do with clouds or lightning; it was the new year that slipped from one time zone to the next, again and again igniting people's enthusiasm, making them set off firecrackers, shoot off rockets, down glasses of champagne, and look for places to jump from. And in that whirlwind of activity, New Year's was no longer a fixed point. It was no longer an absolute around which the patterns of my home made perfect sense.

Over the past two months I had fallen into a new place, a five-hundred-acre farm on the other side of an ocean, and I had followed its rhythms without a thought about consequences. Now, I was surprised to find that something had changed. What I had left behind in Hamburg no longer felt permanent. There were other cities, other countries, where people hinged their life stories on different moments in time, and where my own life could make a different kind of sense. I knew that I would leave the farm in a few weeks, but I also knew that what I'd return to wouldn't hold me in the same way it had before. Sooner or later I would have to set out on my own, and there wouldn't be a mapped-out path but just choices to make. And I hoped on that afternoon out in the field, feet sticking into the air, that my choices would somehow add up, would give me a chance to belong with grace.

The tractor came once more to the end of the field. Once again I pulled the throttle toward the turtle, stepped on the brake, and turned around.

Word Choices

Outside the train window, the lights of Berlin glided past at an even pace. Some of the houses crowded in close enough to the tracks to allow brief glimpses into other people's lives: a family at dinner, a woman rinsing dishes, shadows slipping through the blue flicker of television sets. Renee and I sat across from each other, slumped against our backpacks, tired, filing away memories of our weekend in Prague. When the train reached the next station, a handful of new passengers came trickling in. At this time of day, the car was almost empty, giving everyone a chance to find a private niche. The doors slid shut again, and the train slowly sped up. "Die Fahrkarten bitte." Two men, one at each end of the car, got up from their seats, took out their official badges, and began to check the tickets. I knew these random controls happened on Metro trains, only tonight I could have done without one. I had my Metro pass for my daily trip to work, but Renee's ticket had expired with our arrival at Berlin-Hauptbahnhof. She sat across from me, tired, dreamy, and illegal. In fact, I had told her not to worry about a Metro ticket when we had changed trains at the Hauptbahnhof. It was Sunday night. There would be no ticket inspectors on duty. She would be fine. Nothing to worry about.

"Die Fahrkarten bitte." I took out my Metro pass, and the man in the blue parka nodded briefly. Renee was next. She handed over her expired ticket without saying a word. The inspector looked at the ticket, and his face curled into a question mark. That was when I started talking. "Entschuldigung, aber we have thought, daß the ticket noch good ist. Hier on the ticket steht doch that we can fahren bis zu die final Bahnhof. Not true? Ich not verstehn. Ist das ticket expired? We sind sorry when das ticket nicht good ist." The inspector's face curled up some more, and he began to look downright unhappy. In a few, slow German sentences he explained to us that we would have to get off at the next station and that there was a sixty-Mark fine for riding without a ticket.

The train stopped at Berlin-Tiergarten and the three of us stepped out onto the empty platform. Right away, I continued my explanation, weaving German and English into a confusing barrage that, after a few more minutes, had the inspector cornered. "Na gut," he said, still speaking slow and deliberate German, "I will let you off this time. But make sure that it doesn't happen again. Get yourself a regular ticket at the automatic teller." He left us standing in the middle of the platform. As soon as he had disappeared, Renee slumped down on one of the benches and burst into laughter. I was pleased. We had saved sixty Marks. And I had convinced a fellow German that I was a confused American tourist.

The pleasure I felt in that moment was partly the intoxication that comes from playing a role, the tingling in the stomach that wells up as one self pours into the outline of another. Besides, I felt slightly giddy from trespassing outside the realm of respectability, from having flirted with whatever criminal energy lurks in the darker corners of my mind. Underneath these pleasures, however, ran a deeper, infinitely more personal one. During the few minutes of talking to the inspector, I had condensed my two languages into one. For a short while, German and English were breathing in unison. Speaking both languages at the same time, I hadn't had to worry, for once, about stuffing the marrow of one language into the bones of another. No translation necessary. I had created a language of my own, and I couldn't go wrong. The rules were mine. The words were mine.

"Home language." I like the sound of those two words together. A couple of months ago, in an article about children who grow up with two languages, I found this phrase used to describe a child's first language, the one spoken around the dinner table or whispered in the attic. When my brother and I lay awake at night in our house in Hamburg, talking back and forth through the bookshelf dividing our room, making up stories that soon turned into dreams, we spoke German. The thought that there were other languages, whispered by other boys before they fell asleep, was a faint abstraction to us, a curious fact belonging to an adult world. Surely, old Frau Russow who lived with her cat in a dilapidated cottage on Maimoorweg, only a few hundred yards from our house, was in reality *eine alte Hexe, die kleine Kinder verzaubert.* And one branch of the pear tree outside our window looked exactly like *eine Ameise mit langen Fühlern, die sich langsam im Wind drehen.* And when our friend Christian got his lip stuck on a Popsicle, his mother took a pair of scissors *und schneidete das Eis in kleine Stücke.* All this existed only in German, which easily made its way through the bookshelf, giving shape to our imaginations.

My brother learned his first English words in Gymnasium. He is four years older than I am, and I remember watching his disgruntled march through the upper grades with a good bit of awe. His books usually lay scattered across his desk, the lack of order showing his disgust with school, Latin and music the two subjects he hated with unlimited passion. To this day, I don't know what he thought about English. Once in a while I would hear him murmur a few English words or see him leaf through his English textbook, and one summer he even went to England for a few weeks. All I ever heard about that trip, listening open-mouthed, was that he lost his virginity in an English bedroom. In the end, Gymnasium didn't manage to contain my brother's energies: he transferred to a professional school, became an apprentice, and today runs the family business in Hamburg, selling an average of twenty thousand cases of beer a day. In the pattern of his life, the intricacies of English grammar must seem remote and static, a theoretical language.

My parents, too, view English from a distance. A few years back, my mother decided to take a couple of English classes. She started out with enthusiasm, carefully wrote her name on the cover of her beginner's textbook, and three weeks later tried to bribe me into doing her homework. What she really wanted from those classes, I think, was a good time with friends, afternoons of distraction from the quiet of her living room. About twenty words have survived from this excursion into English, words that she pulls out in unexpected moments and delivers with a slight giggle. When I'm home for a visit, coming into the house after my parents have gone to sleep, I occasionally find a note on my bedroom door, a few German lines reminding me of an errand

I promised to run in the morning. I read through the note, try to remember, and then find myself stopped by four English words: "Good night, your mother."

Unlike my mother, my father has never gone near a foreign language. He went to work in the Hamburg shipyards when he was fourteen and didn't stop working until last year. Even German, his native language, can leave him uneasy, giving his hands too little to hold on to. The few times he has had to prepare a speech, sitting in his leather armchair with a legal pad, he has looked as hesitant as a first-time skater marooned in the middle of a rink. Sometimes my father overhears me speaking English on the phone. After I hang up the receiver, he will ask me to repeat one or two of the words he remembers. "What was that word you used at the end —*foschnittlie*?" "Oh, you mean *fortunately*. That means *glücklicherweise*." And then he will let the word dance on his tongue, "Foschnittlie, foschnittlie . . . ," as if it were exotic candy full of surprising flavors.

"Home language." One thing the author of the article did not do with this phrase was turn it on its head. A simple switch of the two words creates a new space, a space in which my sense of orientation begins to falter: *language home*. I am not sure where my language home lies anymore. At one point, it was exclusively inside of German, in the company of long composite nouns and verbs that love to nestle up at the ends of sentences. That certainty has disappeared. Four years after my brother, I took my first steps into English. It was a slow beginning with vocabulary lists, writing exercises, and long hours in the language lab. "This is Peter. This is Mary. Peter and Mary are brother and sister." As the words came trickling through the headphones, Frau Hilbert would be scanning us from her desk, the smile on her face an unsure mix of determination and benevolence. I liked the feel of new words: new sounds, as fragile as bird wings, that meant something real in countries I had never seen. Twenty years later, I have followed English all the way to America. I have lived with English on a farm in California, on the Cumberland Plateau in Tennessee, and now in the generous spaces of Iowa. I buy toothpaste in English. I use English to cuss on the tennis court. I write in English. And once, a few years ago, I told a woman that I would marry her. In English.

The line that runs through my language home is not unlike a tripwire, easy to miss but hard to ignore. Whenever I get ready to travel between Germany and America, I pack my bags and slide my passport into a leather pouch I carry around my neck. I have never had any problems getting past the immigration officers on either side of the Atlantic. They ask the routine questions, stamp the arrival date into my passport, and wave me into the country. Crossing the language line is much more perplexing to me. Whatever I attempt to bring from one language to the other, no matter how slowly or carefully I may move, undergoes a peculiar change. Unlike my bags, the words I carry never retain their original shape or weight; they inflate or shrivel up, fly high in the air or plummet to the ground.

Take *pumpkin*, for example. I have seen pumpkins lined up on dark porches, their eyes glowing with a fierce hunger. In those moments, they reminded me of trolls hiding under beds or lurking in closets. I have seen the same pumpkins in daylight and admired their facade of innocence, their clever way of disguising themselves as mere food. In early November, I have seen pumpkins fold in on themselves, as if they too knew the pains of growing old. I have seen pumpkins smashed on sidewalks and found myself thinking of winter. I have fed on pumpkins. I like them best as pie with vanilla ice cream. *Pumpkin* equals *Kürbis* — that is the way I find it in any English-German dictionary. In my mind, that is a lie. Trapped inside of jars, the pale pieces of *Kürbis* that stare at me from the supermarket shelves in Hamburg know nothing about pumpkins. They are quite harmless and blissfully ignorant; they could never imagine a world where vegetables are allowed to trespass among humans.

It happens in the other direction too. If I take *gemütlich* with me across the language line, I end up with *cozy*. But a house that is cozy is not the same as a house that is *gemütlich*. Some things I am likely to find in both places: an armchair that fits the curve of my back, a fire that chases shadows across the walls, the smell of tea with a shot of rum, and maybe the shameless yawn of a beagle. And yet, *gemütlich* reaches beyond *cozy*; it isn't satisfied with describing the pleasant atmosphere created by the right combination of external objects. *Gemütlich* wants more; it wants to take the armchair, the fire, the beagle and weave them into my *Gemüt*, my mind, my feeling, my temper. *Gemütlich* takes the room and me, slides us into a blender, and whirls us around until we are one — a feat that *cozy* can only dream about.

The result of these disturbances at the language line is silence. I don't actually become speechless. That is not the problem. Sitting with my parents in their living room, coffee and cake in front of me, I answer their questions about my life in America. Even after eight years, they are not sure about this place their son has disappeared to. The English words my father tries out on occasion and my mother puts into her notes are like brief expeditions toward this place, quick sound waves they send out in the hope of catching a sharper image. My answers travel across the coffee table, and I am half surprised by the fluidity with which I string German sentence after German sentence. "*Wie interessant*," my mother says, nodding her head, unaware of all that doesn't get told. The tiny pieces of silence hanging between *pumpkin* and *Kürbis* or *gemütlich* and *cozy* multiply with all the other silences until the story I tell has a gaping hole in it. Something doesn't translate, something slips away the moment I put it into words. My mother nods, reaches across the table, and slides another piece of cake onto my plate.

Three weeks ago, over Labor Day weekend, I was leafing through a stack of old postcards in an antique store. A few friends and I had driven into McGregor, Iowa, to escape from the rain that was drenching our tents in a small park not far from the Mississippi. McGregor's Main Street is home to some six or seven antique stores that sell everything from old saddle blankets to 1950s *Life* magazine ads. While I was trying to decide whether some of the postcards had actually been written by the store owner, my friend John began talking to another visitor.

"Looks like the rain caught you by surprise too, hey?"

"Yeah, pretty miserable out there." The woman who answered belonged to a group of bikers we had seen riding into town earlier. One by one, they had filed past us, headlights on, engines bellowing in low gears, a dazzling procession. "Not much you can do in this kind of weather," she said. "So we decided to check this place out; do a little antiquing and see what happens."

There wasn't much more to the conversation. Just two people being friendly in a place neither had expected to be. I am sure I would have forgotten about this woman by now, if it hadn't been for that word she used: *antiquing*. I had never come across that word before. To hear *antique* grow into a verb was a bit like seeing a traffic cop dance in the middle of an intersection. The odd thing was it made complete sense. Somehow it felt right that this woman who rode a Harley Davidson and wore a leather jacket with tassels would come to McGregor to antique. It was as if the speed with which she rode her cycle and made her tassels flutter in the wind had found a way into her language. As if the constant movement of pistons, chain, and wheels had leaped into her nervous system, had found a path to the left side of her brain, to that secret place where words are stored and sometimes made.

I am sure that the woman in McGregor wasn't the first person to breathe new life into *antique*. The speed with which nouns become verbs in America has always astounded me. On one day, people strive to have an impact. A day later, they strive to impact. It is as if nouns in America fail to fulfill a basic desire for movement and fluidity. On July 12, 1893, a young American historian read a paper at the Columbian Exposition in Chicago that had a lot to say about movement. I imagine the thirty-one-year-old Frederick Jackson Turner was nervous when he told his older colleagues that they had it all wrong. American society, he told them, wasn't a flowering of European seeds. The structure of American society had its roots at the frontier, where social roles were nothing but a dress rehearsal, where people moved only to move again. By now, a good many historians have taken a bite out of Turner's "frontier thesis," but nobody seems willing to discard it completely. And I wonder whether Turner, without knowing it, wasn't as much a linguist as he was a historian. Maybe all that movement he described wasn't just the source of political institutions and laws, but also the source of a language intoxicated with change. With each move, English had to move also; it had to find words for new landscapes and experiences, and all this with the combined imagination of Europe looking over its shoulder, hungry to hear about the sounds, smells, and spaces at the heart of this New World. Who knows whether the constant need to fill the unfamiliar with words hasn't survived in the ability to "do a little antiquing?"

What I do know for sure is this: I speak English, and English speaks me in return. Thought and language don't exist in a clear-cut hierarchy; they are as interdependent as the different parts of a mobile. And each language, tied to the history of a people, lets the mobile dance in a slightly different rhythm. When I speak English, my thoughts are assembled with the tools English provides. And if one of the tools is a hammer with which I can shape a noun into a verb, then I may have that kind of thought: a thought sliding from stasis into movement, a thought catching the first scent of an action, a thought falling forward like a perched bird preparing to defy gravity. When I speak German, I use a different set of tools with a different history. My parents keep a picture of our family tree in their living room. It is a large oak tree whose roots reach back to 1603. On this tree, I am a tiny twig in the upper left-hand corner, hardly visible without a magnifying glass. Most of the people on this tree stayed put, never venturing far beyond the boundaries of northern Germany. Over the centuries, the language of my ancestors has developed its own rhythm, its own way of making sense of the world. Inside that language, my thoughts find different spaces, flirting with a different kind of potential.

The only time I had to baby-sit in my life, filling in for a friend here in America, I was in charge of two brothers. The older boy was about seven, the younger one must have been around three. They were friendly little fellows who didn't give me much trouble. What made the baby-sitting a lot more entertaining than I had expected was the younger brother. He talked a blue streak, but none of his sentences made any sense. He had perfectly natural intonation, some of his sentences sounded like orders, others like questions, but not a single word he uttered was English. His parents had become worried enough about their son's verbal escapades to consult a speech therapist, who had told them to be patient. "Seg lapom tild holl bomlum ta feal?" the little boy would ask, pointing to a picture on the wall. At first, I wasn't sure what to do. Before his parents had left for the evening, they talked to him just as they did to the older son. I decided to take the other route. "Sis trog lapom spol tum gebo," I tried as an answer. His face lit up; he seemed to understand. For the rest of the evening, we stuck to our language and we agreed on everything.

It didn't strike me until a few days ago that I talked to the little boy in much the same way I lied to the ticket inspector on that Sunday night in Berlin. In both cases, I jumped at the chance of having a new language, a language whose reach was limitless, a kind of private Esperanto. Though I have always been amused by the idealists who meet in some remote language lab to create a universal language, lately I have found that project much less peculiar. It would be nice to sit down with my friend John in Iowa City and tell him, in a language we truly share, what it looks like when the fog lifts off the river in my hometown. Or to tell my friend Ralf in Hamburg about the size of the sky on an Iowa summer day. Or, and this would be a luxury indeed, to have a language in which my parents and my brother could always read the words I write.

Houses

About fifteen miles north of the Alabama border, in Hot Rock, Tennessee, surrounded by grassy hills and patches of trees, past an old goat barn, at the end of a short dirt road, sits a house without ceilings. A few years ago, I lived in this house for the better part of a week to visit with friends. The house was new back then, taking final shape, its future porch a mere outline on a level piece of grass, the frame of the winter garden half finished, clinging to the southern wall like a set of delicate fingers. Inside the house, most of the work had been finished. When I stepped through the front door, I knew I had never before entered a house like this one. In fact, I realized I had never before entered a house. All I had done in the past had been to walk into rooms, boxes of privacy sitting on top of and next to each other. This was different. As soon as I had crossed the threshold, I stared in disbelief at the gargantuan skin of a house, all of it one space, and I bent my neck until I could see the roof resting on its rafters.

The ground floor stretched out in front of me with the loose charm of a furniture store. On the right, couch, recliners, and a TV set contracted into a kind of living room. Behind it, a bed and a couple of dressers marked the room of the oldest son. Across from the bedroom corner, the kitchen spread its appliances along the northern wall. Next to the kitchen area sat the dining table with eight chairs, and next to the dining table was the living room, where my eyes had started out. Between living room and bedroom corner, a flight of wooden stairs led up to a small platform in front of a panorama window (you could see the old goat barn from here). And another flight of stairs led from the platform to a wooden catwalk giving access to the second-floor bedrooms. Walking along the catwalk, I could look down into living room, bedroom, kitchen, and dining room like an archeologist staring into the geometry of his dig. None of the rooms on the second floor, including the bathroom, had a ceiling; they too allowed the eyes to roam upward, higher and higher, into the watery shadows underneath the roof.

To live in this house, even if only for a few days, felt like stumbling from wakefulness into the texture of dreams, diving in and out of spaces that weren't supposed to exist. Whatever rooms I had stored in my head didn't match up with the one room I was in now. Standing in the shower my first morning, letting the hot water run down my back, I sent up clouds of hot steam that found no ceiling and didn't return to paste their water across the bathroom mirror. All of the steam flew up toward the roof, taking pieces of my sleep between the rafters, stretching my slow awakening into what should have been an attic, full of trunks, worn-out boots, and cobwebbed toboggans. In this house, the washcloth in my hand grew heavy with possibilities. It looked like a new thing, connected by invisible trajectories to the couch downstairs, to the pillow in my bedroom, to the flowers on the dining room table. For a second or two, I was tempted to fling the washcloth out of the shower stall and see where it would land, in what part of the house it would intrude with soap and water.

At night, sounds traveled through the house without effort. I could hear the islands of breathing spread out evenly around me. And the longer I listened — my own breathing falling in with the others — the more it was the house itself that seemed to breathe, inhaling, holding the air, exhaling, the walls touching again at ninety-degree angles. One night it rained, a spring storm coming down hard on the metal roof. Without an attic or anything else to muffle the sound, the raindrops came down like heavy coins, hammering and scratching, impatient with their interrupted journey to the ground. House and roof held, as I knew they would, but they did so with humility, guarding me with a single layer of wooden skin, a permeable membrane that didn't deny the wind, the rain, or the surrounding hills. A stray sparrow fluttering in through the door by accident, its wet wings brushing against the desk lamp, wouldn't have looked out of place here. I listened to the rain for another hour or so, admiring the work of the roof, and then fell asleep.

"For our house is our corner of the world. As has often been said, it is our first universe, a real cosmos in every sense of the word." This is what French philosopher Gaston Bachelard writes about houses in

The Poetics of Space. For him, houses are more than three-dimensional conveniences; in the interplay of mind and architecture, they rise around us like the outermost layer of our bodies, creating spaces in which our imaginations can take shape and grow, in which a self can stretch its limbs and begin to grasp its own dimensions. Houses — full of rooms, windows, corners, nooks, crannies, alcoves, hallways, attics, and basements — feed our minds with metaphorical possibilities; they give us a language for expressing our sense of identity.

Think of houses in fiction. What writer does not, at some point, give a character's inner life the visibility of joints, studs, and rafters? Edgar Allan Poe's short story "The Fall of the House of Usher" is all about this connection between house and man. The Usher mansion with its "bleak walls," "vacant eyelike windows," and eaves overgrown by fungi is nothing else but Roderick Usher's morbidity turned solid. Usher and his house become one sentient being in this story, living and dying together like Siamese twins, making the horrified narrator jump on his horse and flee the scene. Henry James in *The Portrait of a Lady* moves Isabel Archer through a series of houses, framing her in doorways like a precious diamond, and each house Isabel enters is full of clues about herself or the people she meets. Or take Kate Chopin's *The Awakening*. When Edna Pontellier tires of house and husband, their staid respectability, she packs her belongings and moves into the "pigeon-house" — a much smaller place, somewhat neglected, with a door opening directly into the parlor. The simplicity of the new space captures the woman Edna is becoming, the one she feels stirring inside, the one who will test the reach of her independence.

House and mind form a pair, again and again, the latter snatching a language from the former. Psychologists, like writers, have long since made good use of this link. They put a sheet of paper in front of a child and request, as if it all were just a game, a picture of a house. What they secretly hope for, of course, is a mind print, a map to guide them along the paths of fear and desire. But houses do more than groom our minds. Being solid, they also train our bodies. Bachelard reminds us that each house we live in seeps into our movements, giving us a muscular memory of all its architectural idiosyncrasies — the third step of the stairs that is higher than all the others, the window on the second floor that only slides open at an angle, the weight of the entrance door, the shape of the kitchen counter, the width of door frames. All of this information collects in our muscles like water running into a jug. A friend of mine once found himself in a motel room whose beds stood alongside the walls, ninety degrees out of place from all the other motel beds he had slept in over the years. When he woke up in the middle of the night, he swung his feet out of bed, stood up, yawned, and walked straight into the wall.

The house I grew up in in Germany sits on Maimoortwiete, a tiny side street in Bramfeld, one of Hamburg's more or less respectable middle-class neighborhoods. My grandfather Hans began building the house in 1966, and it took him about a year to get the job done. Money was tight, and being a traditional northern German businessman who cherished his independence as much as a good cigar, my grandfather had no intention of going into debt. Whenever money came in, he hired construction workers, and the house went through another growth spurt, its brick walls edging a bit closer toward the sky. He picked two colors for the outside bricks: dark brown and yellow. The brown bricks are close to the ground and rise no higher than five feet before making room for the yellow ones. I still wonder about these two colors, not sure whether my grandfather had for once succumbed to an aesthetic decision or whether he had worried about the lower bricks getting dirty. When the last few bricks were slipped into place in the spring of 1967, the new house stood two stories high, one side connected to my grandfather's own house, the other side overlooking the family business — a beer and beverage wholesale company. The house had two apartments, and my parents moved into the upstairs one, their new life suspended between the roar of beer trucks and parental advice.

To get to our part of the house, I had to climb a short flight of stone stairs to the main door, and from there a second, longer flight to our apartment. This second flight led through an entrance hall whose stone floor and tiled walls produced a fine echo. When I tied my shoelaces at the top of the stairs, I would often whistle some made-up tune just to hear it dance with itself. Or I would shout and then listen to the muffled response that seemed to come up from the basement. Somewhere down there, I imagined, behind a door we hadn't found yet, lived a boy my age, who rode wild horses and talked to wizards. The echo was also a good alarm system because it made it easy to hear footsteps. If my brother and I had fought and trashed our room, we could tell from the rhythm of footsteps what needed to be done. My mother's slow, uneven steps gave us enough time to clean up most of the mess we had made. But my father's swift staccato allowed us only to tuck in our shirts and work on our facial expressions. We usually tried innocence with a touch of pleasant surprise.

My brother and I shared a small room with one large window, which had a good view of my grandparents' garden. We could see the half-moon shaped patch of manicured roses, the lanky sunflowers, and the row of tall poplars and birch trees, which formed a green wall in the summer and stood like flagpoles in the winter. On cold days in December or January, I would sometimes pull up a chair to the window, stick my feet between the radiator pipes, and look out over the garden. A red-brick house, invisible during the summer, now shimmered through the tree branches. I liked the view of the garden, its winter mood, and I also liked the red house, mostly because of an old woman who fed seagulls from her window. She would stand at the windowsill on clear winter days, a basket of bread in front of her, and begin to throw crumbs into the air. Within minutes a flock of seagulls would appear, white bodies shooting up and down, flying tight curves, standing still, flapping, screaming, tumbling, chasing each other, and never once touching the house.

Since our apartment was upstairs, well within the roof, most of our rooms had slanted walls. I liked the slant, even though it sometimes made it hard to hang posters. One year, my brother gave me a British flag after his trip to England. I loved it, not knowing that what he had really given me was a dishtowel that looked like a Union Jack. Every other week or so I would wrestle the flag against the slant with the help of four needles, the only thing my mother let me use on the wallpaper. Each time, gravity won out. Still, I liked the slant, the atmosphere it created. Somehow it assured me of the roof, whispered that I was in a secure place far above the ground. And at the same time, it managed the opposite, wrapping me into a kind of subterranean coziness that spilled over into my dream of a large cave with all our furniture neatly arranged.

Despite our apartment's intrusion into the roof, we still had room for an attic. Its door sat in the ceiling of our hallway, and there would be a loud screech when I opened the door with a pole and unfolded the metal ladder. This was always a moment of crisis for my mother, who despised the ladder as much as she would have an overgrown spider leg coming down on her carpet. For a while, we took frequent trips into the attic because a marten had decided to move in and refused to leave. We could hear him running around at night. As we grew more tired, he grew more restless. Around midnight, his antics climaxed in a wild dance, full of brief sprints and what sounded like cartwheels of bone and muscle. We set up a number of traps, some more evil than others, but for a long time the marten stayed ahead of us, thrashing and clawing, oblivious to our contraptions. Finally, we found a way to make him pack up: an electronic signal, inaudible to humans but deafening to marten ears. Within a couple of weeks, the attic fell silent again and my mother no longer dreaded nightfall.

Of all the houses I have lived in over the past thirty years, the one on Maimoortwiete sits deepest in my mind and muscles; it is the place where my idea of a house begins. But this idea has become muddled in my head. When I first left Hamburg for America, I made an effort to come prepared. I expected another language, different food, customs, climate, and landscape. But for some reason I forgot about houses. I never expected walls, windows, roofs, and porches to turn into surprises that would make me look again at how we take shelter from the world. Cynthia Ozick writes that "nothing shakes the heart so much as meeting — far, far away — what you last met at home." This change of the ordinary into the extraordinary, Ozick says, turns travelers into ontologists—investigators of the nature of being, who marvel like children at teapots and stones. I am familiar with these symptoms. In my mind, houses have become marvelous again; they are like playgrounds where body, self, and space chase each other in wild abandon.

Like all ontologists, I find the simplest observations the most breathtaking: A house separates inside from outside. Having lived among two sets of houses, an ocean apart from each other, this observation unfolds in my mind like ancient wisdom. Surely, American houses keep inside apart from outside. And German houses can't help but do it too. But they don't do it in the same way. One by one, American houses add up to an architectural universe whose inside is different from the inside created by German houses. I'm not complaining. Both sets of houses have been perfectly accommodating. They have given me places to keep my feet warm, eat breakfast, shower, read books, write letters, sleep, make love, all the things you expect a decent house to do for you. What differs is the line they draw between inside and outside. What differs is how they offer me to the world and the world to me.

I still remember the shock I felt when a house, cut in half and strapped onto two trucks, rolled past me on a highway in Florida. Less than ten feet from my steering wheel, a brand-new door and porch light invited me to enter, and for a brief moment I expected a face to appear in one of the windows. The open sides of the house had been covered with tarps that bulged in the wind like spinnakers. In some places, the tarps had broken loose, fluttering frantically, and I could hear their mad complaints mixing with the sounds of my radio. A house, cracked in halves, moving through the countryside at fifty miles an hour — there was something profoundly disturbing about this picture. It didn't feel right; it was unpleasant, like watching someone undress you had no intention of seeing naked. If there is such a thing as spatial etiquette, then it was being ignored that day in Florida. How can a house recover from a road trip?

That day in Florida, I realized there are degrees of inside. It was the first glimpse of what I now know for sure: Many American houses court the outside. They create a space that is less absolute, more fragile than the one I'm used to. This is biased, of course. If I had been raised a Tuareg in a leather tent halfway between Ghat and Timbuktu, American houses would feel like fortresses to me. But I happened to grow up in Hamburg, in northern Germany, in northern Europe, in short, in one of the cradles of domestic architecture. According to architect and historian Witold Rybczynski, the Dutch, who live a stone's throw from Hamburg, fell in love with their houses in the seventeenth century. While most of Europe was still rural, the affluent Dutch became townspeople, turning their brick houses into snug havens, which, for the first time in history, blended the idea of house and home on a larger scale. Dutch houses became intimate, separating home life from work life. They provided shelter, but they also provided a space in which a family's history could grow with the slow determination of ivy. Foreign visitors to these houses were surprised when asked to remove their shoes or put on slippers before coming upstairs. And they were even more surprised when they saw, in one of the living room corners, a detailed scale model of the very house they had just entered, a kind of domestic shrine that celebrated the family's affection for their home. My geographical roots, then, make me a creature of houses, a brick dweller, who sees no link between houses and highways, who thinks of houses and then thinks of staying put.

Whenever there was enough snow on the ground, the brick walls along Maimoortwiete turned into giant target ranges. Our favorite target was the southern wall of the apartment building across the street. It was the highest one around and almost completely without windows. Rainer, Jens-Peter, Christian, Olaf, my brother, and I would line up and start flinging our snowballs. The goal was to leave the highest mark, which, on a perfect day, meant hitting the pointed top of the gable. No one could go higher than that. Snowball after snowball flew against the wall, exploded, and fell back down on us like fresh snow. Since we all threw at once, we usually had a couple of fights about who could claim one of the better marks. But the fights never lasted long, because we were too hungry for motion, for scooping up the snow, packing it, once, twice, and then releasing it with all our strength, the perfect arc already mapped out in our heads. When we got tired, our arms tingling from exhaustion, some two hundred white dots would cling to the wall. Later in the afternoon, I would be able to retrace the competition from our living room window with a cup of hot chocolate in front of me. In the growing twilight the dots began to glow like low-voltage bulbs against the red of the bricks, and if I let my mind slip just a little farther into drowsiness, I could believe that we had really been up there, stringing Christmas lights where nobody else dared to climb.

There were other games in the summer. When it was too hot to move around much, we took pieces of flint stone and engraved the bricks with our names and fast shifting loyalties, our faces close to the wall, the day's heat thrown back at us, the dry smell of bricks in our noses. On cooler days, we played *Bulle Lauf*, a chase around the block, which always started and ended by touching the same stretch of wall next to an old drainpipe. Since I was one of the youngest, I never did too well in this game. Once in a while, though, an older boy would feel cocky and double my head start. Then I had a real chance, and as we cut around the corners and my head start began to melt, all I could think about was that patch of bricks next to the drainpipe, the one place that promised to set me free.

The real surprise American houses have held in store for me isn't the occasional house on the highway; it is their indifference to bricks. American houses unsettle me with their loyalty to wood. Not too long ago, a new apartment building went up in my neighborhood in Iowa City, and I had to walk past the construction site almost every day on my way to work. The first couple of months were pretty uneventful, mostly ground work and the pouring of foundations. Next came the parking area, a thing of steel and concrete, on top of which the actual building would sit as if on a stage. The day the carpenters came in and started putting up the wood frame, I began to slow down my steps. It wasn't the first time this happened to me. Whenever I see an American house rise up like a skeleton of wood, I can't help staring. What catches my attention is the dance of house and landscape: I can see studs and rafters; I can see the shape of rooms and windows; but I can also see land and sky. I can look right through the house and choose to ignore it.

There is a short time in the life of an American house, right before the sheathing gets nailed into place, when it both is and is not, when inside and outside are one. The new apartment building was no different, and I looked at it for several days, letting my imagination play along its unclear boundaries. Up there, some ten feet off the ground, the wood frame did look like a stage set, and the carpenters already seemed to know their parts, passing through the walls like so many belted ghosts. No house on Maimoortwiete has ever played such games. Right from the start, a brick house is all business. It cherishes its growing privacy with each layer of brick the mason slips into place. But many American houses come, at least once, to that point of uncertainty, when they forget their aspirations and let in the land.

The house I live in now, an odd accumulation of rooms built over the stretch of a century, hides its wood frame under steel siding and a handful of fake granite rocks. For the longest time I thought the rocks were real until, one winter, I kicked them hard with my snow-covered boots and heard the hollow ring of plastic. In the end, it doesn't much matter what gets built around the wood frame — plastic, aluminum, steel, or even real stone. Inside my house, and inside most American houses, I can never quite shake the image of the wood frame, its airy structure that keeps reminding me of a world outside. What also stays in my mind is the memory of wood itself. To build with wood is to build with an appreciation of the sky. Wood knows about gathering landscape into spaces; it knows about movement and the intricate play of light and shadow. Wood, containing the stuff of life, has caught a glimpse of transience.

In all this, wood differs from bricks, which look down instead of up. Bricks belong to the earth — the cool, tranquil darkness under our feet. They don't bother with animation; there is nothing fickle about them as they wait for time itself to run its course. Bricks want permanence, and so do the houses they build.

A couple of months into my first long stay in America, I had to demolish a house in California. Back then I was working as a field hand for Don Brown, a thoughtful man with hands the size of plowshares, who owns a five hundred–acre farm in the San Joaquin Valley. One day, Don decided it was time to take down the small wooden house that had been standing abandoned near his driveway for a number of years. Equipped with crowbars and hammers, we set to work early in the morning. It was easy to yank off the outside boards, and soon a couple of gaping holes appeared in the walls. We kept at it for about a week, scurrying around the house like termites, gnawing away the walls until the house was nothing but a handful of studs tottering under the weight of the roof.

I felt a growing tension during that week of work, waiting, I guess, for the house to put up a fight. It had been built in the 1920s, and there were subtle reminders of the people who had lived in it over the years — layers of wallpaper, tiny dents in the floorboards, a couple of rusty tin cans under the kitchen sink, coat hangers, a piece of yellow curtain. The more I used my crowbar and hammer, the more I felt like an intruder, tearing apart a fine-spun web of memories clinging to the inside of the house. Ripping away board after board, I flooded the house with amnesia, a soundless invasion that was the source of my uneasiness. At the end of the week, we hooked up a steel cable between two tractors and pulled it through the house. The few studs we had left standing folded like twigs, and the roof slid to the ground with awkward, mossy defiance.

Then, I did something odd. I found a piece of wood in the pile that used to be a house — it was the hanger rod from the built-in closet — and began to carve it with my pocketknife. Three nights in a row I sat next to the stove in the farmhouse and carved the rod, patiently, into a sword. I hadn't carved anything since my childhood, and the sudden desire to do it again was as surprising to me as it was to Don's wife, who watched me from the kitchen, wondering when I would clean up the shavings. When the sword was finished, the handle an elaborate sequence of squares and pyramids, I took sandpaper and smoothed out whatever edges I could find. Now, fifteen years later, the sword is still around, sitting on a shelf near the stove. On my visits to the farmhouse, I always take it off the shelf and, for a moment or two, engage an imaginary foe. I'm not exactly sure why I carved the sword, but I have a hunch: It was the act of a brick dweller, of someone who refused to see a house and its history disappear without a struggle. And when I play with the sword, slicing through the air and making Don laugh, the house is there again, on the other side of the driveway, chock-full with memories.

A few summers ago, I returned to Maimoortwiete for a visit. It was early August, a sunny, flawless day, and I decided to write a letter to a friend in Iowa. I took my pen, my clipboard, and a glass of orange juice and sat down on the front stairs of our house. After a while, I took off my shoes and rested my feet on the warm stones. When my mother rode up on her bicycle half an hour later, she saw me sprawled out in the sunshine and frowned. "Do you have to sit here like this?" she murmured, stepping around my sheets of paper. She didn't approve of the way in which I had dragged the letter writing (orange juice and no shoes included) into the open; it was as if she had discovered a hole in the facade of her house through which her son had fallen by accident.

My mother's frustration made me think, and by the time she had closed the door behind her, I knew where I had gone wrong: I had built a porch without knowing it. I had taken a foreign space and slipped it on our house. There are no porches on Maimoortwiete or anywhere else in Hamburg. The houses I grew up with have patios, balconies, and large windows that open like wings, but they don't hand over their privacy on porches, where passersby can take a good long look, where their eyes can almost find the inside. The houses I grew up with prefer an uncluttered facade, a space of dignified silence and stillness that marks the threshold of a home. And not one of them has a front door that leads directly into a living room. There is always some kind of hall first, a space in which windblown visitors can calm down.

My mother wasn't the only one to notice my transgression that day. The neighbors, who happened to walk past our house, also didn't expect to find me where I was. I startled them like an apparition, a letter-writing ghost, and for a short moment they didn't know how to compose themselves. They tried to put on their public faces, to nod or smile, but the seams were showing — traces of other selves scrambling for cover. My spatial confusion, which had brought me to the stairs, in turn confused my neighbors, and in the midst of it all we had a chance to see each other new. And soon I wasn't writing my letter, but I found myself thinking about Herr Eggers, who seemed to fall backward when he walked and once went to Thailand to find himself a wife. And Frau Pinnow, who used to cut my hair in her kitchen and still had the ready laugh of a girl. I ended up staying on the stairs for a long time. Only when my feet slipped into the growing shadow of a tree did I pack up and move inside.

The longer I commute across an ocean and live in two sets of houses, the more I learn that confusion has a benevolent side. It can be a thick fog that makes you go blind and narrow, but it can also rattle you just enough to widen your field of vision. My mind and muscles have begun to play with the houses that surround them. I can build a porch by sitting down and a whole house by swinging a sword. The spaces around me are moving, granting me unexpected vistas. And if space does indeed connect to self, then, surely, this bodes well.

Niemandsland

The first time I hear about the Wall coming down, I am standing in a cafeteria line in Iowa. Richard, a friend from the music department, gets in line behind me, taps on my shoulder, and wants to know how I feel about "the whole thing." I am the only German he knows on campus, and he is anxious to hear the opinion of a native. I smile when I hear his question and continue to look at the menu. I am not sure whether I should get the spaghetti and play it safe or whether to risk the boiled fish. Obviously, Richard is in a good mood today. He always cracks jokes and makes up stories when things are going well with his piano playing. I decide in favor of the spaghetti. Few cafeterias are bad enough to spoil pasta dishes. Richard looks at me in amazement.

The Wall was built in 1961. I was born in 1965. For me, and for most of my friends at home, the Wall had always existed — a forty-kilometer slab of concrete, twisting its way through Berlin from north to south, one side smeared with graffiti, a convenient target for soccer balls and last resort for poodles without a tree, the other side all somber gray, barbed wire, and nervous young men with machine guns. But the Wall was only a small part of the border between East and West Germany, a tiny fraction of the hundreds of kilometers that had to be secured in the years following World War II. The rest of the border outside Berlin didn't have the symbolic solidity of a wall; the rest of the border was a three-meter-high wire fence that climbed hills, cut through forests, and followed rivers with the tenacity of a hunting dog.

One such river was the Elbe, which arises in the Giant Mountains of the Czech Republic. After a long loop to the south, it flows in a northwesterly direction and empties its dark brown water into the North Sea. For about ninety kilometers, between Wittenberge and Lauenburg, the Elbe marked the border between East and West Germany. The exact borderline lay in midstream — a bureaucrat's idea, no doubt, hatched out at a conference table under fluorescent light. How do you cut a river in half? The answer is simple: you can't. Instead, you build a fence as close to the river as possible, tracing the shoreline with barbed wire, watchtowers, and spring guns.

I knew this stretch of the fence well. My parents' country house sits tucked away under a large oak tree about a mile west of the Elbe. Each summer I would take countless trips to the river; there was no other place in which summer condensed so easily and completely. The pastures by the river had room for playing Frisbee and flying kites. Between the pastures, narrow sand roads provided the perfect terrain for bicycle races. The river itself held the promise of fish, if I had enough patience and remembered to watch my bobber carefully. Cranes stalked the shoreline. Toads sat in the grass like breathing rocks. And there was the fence — about three hundred meters away, on the other side of the river, with neither beginning nor end. It clung to the river like a special kind of reed, tall, upright, impenetrable. I saw the fence each time I came to the river, and each time I forgot about it, accepted its presence just as I accepted the freighters whose names I tried to read from the shore.

On summer weekends our river town often filled with visitors. They would arrive in their freshly washed cars and make their way to the small harbor at the end of Main Street. Here, they would spill out over the pier, blotches of white, yellow, green, blue, many of them with binoculars dangling from their necks. What attracted them was not the row of motorboats anchored in the harbor or the breeze that whipped across the water; the main attraction was the fence and the watchtower on the opposite shore. Some of the visitors brought cameras instead of binoculars, but whatever they brought, they soon huddled together at the edge of the pier, gazing at the fence that contained another version of Germany.

When I began to understand the history that had strung a fence across my summers, I would occasionally join the crowd at the harbor. These trips to the harbor were not unlike trips to the zoo, filled with hopes of seeing something exotic or dangerous, something that would flick its tail and growl. With my father's binoculars, I would scan the tiny platform of the watchtower until one of the soldiers' faces would spring into focus. No matter what the expression on the soldier's face,

I knew he belonged to one of two categories: Either he secretly longed to be on my side of the fence, had already drawn up plans for his escape on cheap paper, his wife nervous about the packed suitcases in the toolshed, or he had requested border duty out of conviction, his wife using extra starch whenever she cleaned his uniform, his children dressed in blue for another Socialist youth parade. My judgments came easily as I shifted my weight from one foot to the other, my arms slowly getting tired from holding the binoculars.

They watched us too, of course, checking our movements from the watchtower. If the group of West German gazers had grown sufficiently large, a colorful Sunday afternoon crowd in search of entertainment, our ghoulish curiosity was sometimes rewarded with a gesture from the other side. A jeep would appear out of nowhere and drop off a handful of soldiers right behind the fence, each of them holding a pair of binoculars or a camera. Then we began to watch each other in earnest, an odd test of endurance, as if we could convey our contempt for each other through the sheer strength of our vision, as if taking pictures of each other meant taking prisoners. Clad in our respective ideologies, we tried nothing less than to watch each other out of existence.

Over time, the fence and its rituals seeped into my thinking. They were no longer something to wonder about; they simply were. Richard, tapping on my shoulder in the cafeteria line, doesn't know any of this. He doesn't know that his question about the collapse of the Wall is a question I cannot understand in principle. I have followed the news about Germany. I know that thousands of people have been demonstrating in the streets of Leipzig, Dresden, and Halle. But to believe the Wall has come down, and with it the fence, is a mental feat I cannot accomplish for the moment. I put my plate of spaghetti on the tray and walk out into the dining hall. Richard stays right behind me, protesting that he has told me the truth.

Five weeks later I'm on a plane to Germany. I had not planned to return for Christmas, but the events of November 9, 1989, have reshuffled my priorities. The passport I pack for the trip tells me I'm a citizen of the Federal Republic of Germany. That is no longer true. Although there hasn't been legislation yet and nobody knows what the final outcome will be, the country I was born in has disappeared.

"How about a walk before dinner?" My father puts his paper down and points to the window. "Looks like the sun has come out." I nod and push myself up from the sofa. "I'll tell Mom." My mother barely looks up from the stove; two pots of red cabbage have steamed up the small kitchen, and she refuses to leave our Christmas dinner at this crucial stage. "Go right ahead, but be sure to come back in time. Andreas and Christiane are coming at four."

My parents and I arrived at the country house two days ago. Over the past few years, my parents have preferred to spend the holidays in the country rather than the city. They enjoy the slow pace of the village and the certainty that no surprise visitors will show up at the door. My father and I don't take long to decide where our walk should take us. For several days the news shows have called attention to the 24th of December — the first day for West Germans to enter East Germany without a visa. My father has heard rumors about a ferry running again between our village harbor and the other shore. I find it hard to believe, but I want to see for myself.

Forty-five years ago, at the end of World War II, that ferry had a falling out with history. The Russian military administration decided to strengthen the borders of its occupied territory, and our village ferry happened to be in the way. It didn't matter that the ferry connected the two halves of one village, that people used the ferry much like they used any other section of Main Street — women came on bicycles, children arrived with scooters, farmers drove up in tractors to plow land they owned across the river. The ferry was soon shut down, cutting a hole into people's lives. It happened in other places too; all along the 1,400 kilometers of border, wooden watchtowers and rolls of barbed wire appeared between trees and across well-worn country roads. Land that used to grow wheat and barley was now plowed and left barren, turning into a large inkpad that recorded footprints rather than fingerprints. Over the years, the rolls of barbed wire became a full-fledged fence, and the wooden watchtowers matured into cement fortresses with searchlights powerful enough to turn night into day. And while the border grew more and more real, the ties of family, friendship, and land slowly eroded, shrinking into memories kept alive inside a quiet longing.

Even though the sun has come out, the day is still cold, and my father and I send up clouds of breath as we follow the small trail leading to the harbor. The trail is a shortcut that runs along the edge of the village, giving us an open view of the fields whose shades of brown are now broken up by patches of snow. It is easy to tell where the river is from the trail. We are not high enough to see the water, but we can see the steel-gray band of the fence making its way through the marshland.

The moment I catch my first view of the harbor, I know the rumors are true. The ferry has docked on the other side of the river; five or six people are walking up the slight incline of the levee toward the fence, where a small group of East German soldiers is standing guard. I have never seen people move in that stretch of green between river and fence. No-man's-land. Their movements are strangely delicate, as if performed in slow motion, governed by a still unfamiliar choreography. Why are they not afraid? Past and present wrestle each other to a stalemate in my mind, and for a second I do not comprehend what I see. There is a hole in the fence. Right below the watchtower, someone has cut away a section of the fence and has filled it with landscape. I stand and watch.

"Let's go across," my father puts his hand on my shoulder, and points to a handful of people waiting at the end of the pier.

A polite murmur of "Guten Tag" welcomes us as we join the group, but nobody talks very much after that. We all watch the ferry leaving the opposite shore and cutting back diagonally across the river. Most of us are overdressed for a ferry ride. Dress pants stick out from under heavy parkas, high heels seek footing on the slippery wood. We are dressed for the privacy of a Christmas celebration, and yet we have all become absorbed by the public spectacle in front of us. The Christmas routines we are coming from or going to take second place behind the ferry, now reaching the halfway point of its journey, floating on the river like a window in time.

The ride across takes less than ten minutes. My father and I stand at the back of the ferry, watching the harbor and the few familiar buildings getting smaller. We don't talk. Too many things are happening at once, our internal compasses spinning in confusion, the images in our heads twisting and bending as if caught in a sudden breeze. I now see the harbor in the same way the East German soldiers have seen it all along. I begin to imagine a summer crowd of West Germans standing at the end of the pier, gazing across, among them a fourteen-year-old boy trying to steady his father's binoculars. It must have been much worse for the soldiers to be on guard duty in the summer than in the winter. Now, the harbor looks almost abandoned, but in the summer it turns into an amusement park full of curious spectators, and sailboats and motorboats weaving their way back and forth on the river. I have no idea how the East German soldiers made it through those summers, watching from behind thick glass with barely enough room to turn around.

The ferry effortlessly cuts through the water, each minute on the river teaching me a new way of measuring space. We are getting closer to the other shore, and I begin to wonder what the rules are. Where are my father and I going? In the whirlwind of images in my head, the memories of another journey come into focus. Years earlier, my father and I took a rare trip together, a four-week tour through America, driving a tiny Avis rental car from Miami to Milwaukee, where one of my father's school friends had settled in the fifties. Neither my father nor I knew much about America. I remember how the heat outside the air-conditioned Miami airport grabbed me, how it shook me, whispering a strange welcome under the shapes of palm trees. Everything felt different, filled with unexpected sound and movement. Half an hour after our arrival, my father and I left the airport in a blue Nissan, carefully following the Florida map we had brought from Germany. We did fine, until a tollbooth blocked our path at the end of an on-ramp. We had hundreds of dollars in bills and traveler checks, but not the forty cents the machine demanded. My father put the car in reverse, glanced at me, and then shot up the hill of manicured grass next to the tollbooth. The car's suspension moaned as we swerved across the grass, and then, with a final leap, we were back on the highway, ready to continue.

As the ferry whirls the Elbe water from brown into white, I try to match the memories of that trip with our ride across the river. Once again, my father and I are edging toward the unfamiliar, only this time we don't have maps. And maps would be of little use anyway, at least those printed in East Germany. It was more than a rumor that East German maps misrepresented the border area, mixing up streets, fields, trails, woods, and lakes until all they offered was the certainty of getting you lost. My father and I still don't talk, and it is in our silence that the ferry ride goes beyond our awkward arrival in America. More is at stake on this river. When we bounced into Florida like pinballs, we were nervous, but we still knew that a few thousand kilometers to the east a place existed whose gravity gave shape to our orbit. In our heads we carried the grid pattern of home, familiar lines crossing at familiar angles, anchoring us with certainty. On this ferry, in the middle of the river, that certainty is beginning to float; the entire grid has begun to move, tipping, reeling, making it difficult to hang on.

"Almost there." My father points to the makeshift ferry landing. As if running a final equipment check, I rush through the images my mind has stored about East Germany. Newspaper articles about daring escapes, stories about people killed along this border, reports about empty warehouses and funny little cars that take ten years to order. And somewhere in this pile of stories I find my old high school teacher, Herr Depenbusch, an enthusiastic man with a large set of keys on his belt. In eleventh grade, Herr Depenbusch spent an entire semester teaching us the finer differences between East and West Germany. It was an honest effort, not overly biased I thought, but what has stayed with me is the geometry of the handouts — scrupulously prepared charts, West German statistics on the left, East German statistics on the right, all neatly kept apart by a straight line in the middle. And now, I am forty yards away from the fence, a section of that fence has disappeared, and next to the opening stand four East German soldiers around what looks very much like a kitchen table.

The ferry engine slows to a murmur, and for the last few yards we drift with the river current until the sound of metal screeching over rocks announces our arrival. It is a short walk from the ferry landing to the top of the levee. My father stays in front of me as we climb the freshly trampled path. "Do you have your passport?" He turns around and holds up his own. I don't, not even my driver's license. And all of a sudden I am worried I won't be able to get through, that the soldiers will turn out to be as rigid as they have always been. In the past, no one would have stood a chance without a passport at an ordinary border crossing. It would have been stupid to show up without papers, an insult to the East German government that would have ended in stern questions and a car turned inside out. A West German newspaper, carelessly thrown into the car's back seat, was enough to cause trouble.

"Guten Tag." My father greets the first guard inside the fence and hands over his papers. The guard has hardly opened the passport before he closes it again.

"Danke," he hands it back. The other three soldiers stand around the table in a half-circle, their eyes wandering out over the river. One of them begins to dig a little hole in the ground with the heel of his boot.

"Guten Tag. I'm afraid I forgot to bring my passport." After I have seen how my father fared, I am less worried about making this confession. The guard looks at me, then opens a metal box in the middle of the table.

"That will be twenty Marks for a day pass." He takes out a small sheet of gray paper, places a stamp on it, and pushes it over to me. I hand him the twenty Marks.

"Danke."

"Danke."

That's it. Just a handful of words pushed back and forth. The whole exchange is so simple, unassuming, almost tentative, that I cannot believe that I have just been ushered into a space I never expected to see. What is missing during our conversation with the soldiers is a blueprint, a set of boundaries that could contain the confusion on each side of the kitchen table. With our political differences growing fuzzy, we can no longer place each other in the black-and-white landscape of opposing ideologies. It is as if the hole in the fence has allowed the colors to run together, confusing our sense of orientation in a landscape turned gray, a new kind of no-man's-land. I don't know who these men are behind the facade of their stiff uniforms. Are we countrymen yet? I have never felt much need to grant them their humanity. But I imagine their bind to be worse. If they believed in defending Socialism along this border, then the fact that I am standing in front of them right now is a slap in their faces. Whatever joy these four soldiers keep hidden behind their blank expressions, some of them may also feel a dizzying sense of betrayal.

"Look at that!" My father waits for me halfway down the levee. There is a second fence about ten meters ahead. This one is lower than the first, and it is cut wide open to let us through to a cobblestone path leading up to the road and a handful of houses. Heavy electric wires run along its top, making this fence the more threatening of the two. Two fences instead of one. Oddly enough, I feel cheated. It bothers me to think that for all these years I have focused my attention on the wrong fence, have hurled my frustration and contempt at a fence that takes second place behind this one, hidden from sight, low, sturdy, and fatal. The second fence also rekindles my fear, putting the old reports about mines, trip wires, and spring guns back into my head. I lower my eyes to the ground and keep them there, carefully choosing what cobblestones to trust with my body.

The smell of cake. Unmistakable. The first house we get to has all the windows thrown open, the door slightly ajar. A few empty benches and tables are set up in front of it. The entire house seems to exude the aroma. I breathe in slowly, savoring the smell as if it were something brand-new, something invented just now. My father and I aren't the only ones lingering on this stretch of road, enjoying the unexpected smell that settles around our heads like a welcome scarf. Several cars are parked on the sidewalk, people waiting alone or in small groups. Some of them have come to pick up ferry travelers. Others seem to have drifted here out of curiosity. No one appears to be in a particular rush. A few yards away from the soldiers, Christmas and the return of the ferry have widened ordinary tolerance. People have time to seek out each other's faces; nobody minds; hands move up to tip hats.

We are not sure what to do. My father nods back to an elderly couple standing next to their small orange car, a Russian Lada. When my father suggested crossing the river, neither of us had given any thought to what we would do on the other side. We had simply wanted to go, as if only a physical journey could prove to us the reality of the other shore after all those years of watching. The old man next to the Lada motions his wife to stay with the car and comes over.

"Would you maybe like a ride to the next village? My wife and I are going back now." He is a tall man, his complexion stuck somewhere between tan and red. Judging by the size of his hands, he is one of the local farmers.

"Well," my father shoots a quick glance at me, "that is very kind of you. How far away is it?"

"Oh, just about three kilometers. Not far at all, and they have a band playing there."

We agree to come along. I immediately feel drawn to this man. Unlike the soldiers, he seems real, three-dimensional, full of answers to questions I want to ask. His wife greets us with a handshake at the car.

The orange Lada is tiny. When I open one of the back doors, I am not sure I will be able to fit. I am six and a half feet tall, and the amount of leg room I see presents a challenge. I lower myself onto the edge of the seat, trying to pull in my legs behind me. I don't want to give the impression that this car isn't large enough for me. Finally, I'm in, my knees almost level with my shoulders. I reach over for the door and pull it shut. Somehow I misjudge the weight of the door; it closes with a thin metallic bang, and the ashtray above the handle flies across the seat like a stray bullet.

There is a brief moment of silence while I grope under the driver's seat. "Can you find it?" The old man looks back over his shoulder. "Sure, I've got it," I mutter with my forehead pressing against my father's knee. I am too embarrassed to look at the old man and spend more time than I really need to fumble the ashtray back into its frame. Normally, I would shrug this off — just a bit of clumsiness, no harm done. But inside this Lada, on this side of the river, I can't. I feel as if the ashtray has started an avalanche of revelations about who I am, has slid me under a magnifying glass above which the old man and his wife whisper back and forth, examining a West German. My slip-up must seem full of arrogant carelessness to these kind people, full of criticism not only of their car but also their way of life.

The old man puts the Lada into first gear and pulls away from the curb. It is only three kilometers to the village. It won't take long. I let my father do the talking.

Red brick houses and well-kept front yards begin to line the road. The car slows down. On any other day, this village would have looked perfectly self-contained, absorbed in its own rhythm, the clean layout of its structures making it easy for the traveler to glide through. Today such indifference is impossible. People are everywhere, on sidewalks, in gardens, in the middle of the road, they talk across fences, discuss over handlebars of bicycles, underlining their words with the swift movement of arms. We slow down even more and pull into a parking lot next to the town hall.

"I will let you out right here." The old man points to the entrance of the building and shuts off the engine. "This is where the band is playing."

"Vielen Dank. And Merry Christmas." My father gets out of the car, but I hesitate for a moment. I would like to say something else, let the couple know I am curious about the lives they have led in this country that is both my own and entirely foreign. I would like them to understand there are not only the monolithic images created by binoculars. But what I want to say gets away from me until it is too large. It folds in on itself, rolls up into a tight ball, too heavy to move.

"Vielen Dank für ihre Hilfe." I get out of the car and follow my father up the stairs.

The first floor of the town hall has been turned into a makeshift coffeehouse. At one end of the room, a three-man band is pumping out dance tunes. But the noise from the tables proves more than a match for its efforts, and the cigarette smoke is dense enough to turn the players into silhouettes. We find a table close to the entrance and order two cups of coffee. Again I am surprised by the exuberance with which people talk, shaping their words with the help of arms, shoulders, eyebrows, whatever is needed. Nobody here discusses politics. The laughter that jumps around and ignites the tables is the kind that comes from stories heard many times before.

My father and I sip our coffee and watch. Again I sense the silence that has traveled with me on the ferry. Everything I see is new; the shape of the coffee cup in my hand is full of surprises. On this side of the river I feel like a child again. I own only fragments of language, raw chunks that do not yet match the life around me. I have no sense of proportion; an ashtray is all it takes to scare me. My father and I sit for another ten minutes, listening, trying to catch bits and pieces of the stories circling around us. Then, we quietly get up and start back to the ferry.

Two days after our first walk into East Germany, my father returns for a second visit. When he comes back hours later, he is carrying a piece of the fence he found near the ferry landing. He goes into the basement, gets a hammer, and nails the barbed wire next to the woodcut in our living room. When he is done, he turns around and smiles at me. "There, that will do."

I am surprised by my father's action, the swift determination with which he puts the barbed wire where everyone can see it. At first, I want to argue with him, tell him he has it all wrong. Who the hell wants to look at that piece of wire? It seems tasteless and crude to hang it in the living room, the gesture of a hunter who revels in his trophies. But I don't say anything. I sit in the armchair and look at the wall. And after a while, I don't find the piece of wire so ridiculous anymore. I get up from the chair and trace the wire with my fingertips; it is cool, and I can feel the pressure from its sharp edges. A bit of green plastic still sticks to one end, leftover insulation, I think, for an electrical hookup.

My fingers follow the entire length of the wire, half anticipating the remnants of an old current, but there is nothing except the texture of metal and plastic. The simplicity of the sensation pleases me, and I begin to understand my father's odd attachment to his find. The wire is tangible proof, something my fingers can read again and again, something to slice through my confusion like a spine, giving my vague hopes a place to hinge on. Maybe this will work. Maybe the two halves of my country, flowing together through the still small openings in the fence, will blend once more. For now, it is just a hope, a leap into a new space — unmapped, full of frightening promise.

Legacy

The devil has a German accent and drives a Mercedes. Of course, no one in Castle Rock suspects that the friendly old man, who simply drives into town one day, is in fact the devil. How could they know? His manners are impeccable, his black car is elegant, and despite his foreign accent, he is full of a gentle wisdom that makes one feel understood. There is a cosmopolitan ease about him that has nothing to do with arrogance; it holds the listener spellbound, flatters him that this man with a carefully groomed mustache could enjoy their conversation. Moreover, the old man promises to be good for Castle Rock. He has bought up the abandoned house on Main Street, right across from the diner, and plans to turn it into a gift shop. He works quickly and diligently, and before long the old house looks new again, proudly proclaiming its recovered purpose with a hand-painted sign — "Needful Things." And so the story unfolds.

They all come. Of course they do; not much happens in Castle Rock. A new citizen and a new store is a double attraction not to be missed. And the wonderful thing is that everyone finds exactly what he or she needs in the old man's shop. An old baseball card, a silver goblet, a tiny porcelain figurine (the same one that fell off the mantel many years ago). No matter how exotic their craving, all visitors come away satisfied, clutching their purchases as the tiny bell ushers them out of the store. The old man is generous too. He doesn't charge much. Why should he? He didn't come to Castle Rock to make money. After all, he is the devil, and his priorities lie elsewhere. With each gift that he wraps up and hands over for just a few dollars, the old man extracts promises from his grateful customers. The boy who gets the baseball card promises to splatter turkey shit over white linen.

The town drunkard agrees to kill a dog. The Catholic priest goes out to puncture tires.

It's masterful work. Each seed of hatred is carefully slipped into the layers of greed and jealousy that have long since softened the foundation of Castle Rock. Finally, like an overripe tomato, the town bursts apart and erupts into chaos: bullets scream across porches, knife blades dance into bodies. Inside the freshly painted house on Main Street, the old man smiles.

I am not particularly fond of horror movies. And I wouldn't have watched this one if a friend hadn't told me about the devil's German accent. That detail had made me curious. I happen to be German, and so, naturally, a devil who has a German accent and drives a Mercedes intrigues me. It intrigues me, but it doesn't surprise me. A devil with an Italian accent in a Fiat would have surprised me. A devil with a French accent in a Citroën would have flabbergasted me. But not a German devil in a Mercedes.

At the end of the movie, Castle Rock barely survives the devil's cunning. Only one man proves to be his match — a former big-city cop who now runs the local police department. Right from the start his upright walk, his straight jawline, and his broad shoulders single him out. He is the man to keep the universe in line. He is not fooled by the old man, he never sets foot into "Needful Things." But one night, as part of his investigation, the officer shoulders his Mag-Lite and breaks into the old man's basement. He wants more information, wants to know what kind of force he is dealing with. To his surprise, the old man turns out to be an avid collector of old newspapers. Pile after pile of papers drifts into the slim beam of light, and headlines become legible. There is something about the Civil War. Hiroshima. And this: "Hitler Conquers Austria."

All of a sudden the kaleidoscope turns, pieces fall into place, and the movie's liquid symbols find their crystallization point. We are no longer underneath the gift shop; we have arrived in the basement of history. The devil's German accent and his choice of car make perfect sense. We know why the devil prefers to wear a long black coat on his rambles through Castle Rock. We also understand why a beautiful German voice sings Ave Maria as two women cut each other up with butcher knives. All of these things make strange sense because of a failed artist who set out to conquer the world in 1939.

I am unsure about this last sentence: *All of these things make strange sense because of a failed artist who set out to conquer the world in 1939*. I chose this sentence because it seemed to go well with the rest of the paragraph, continuing the lyrical playfulness as it slides into the realm of the real. But now I wonder whether the sentence was such a good choice. I wonder whether it doesn't simplify too much. Someone might read this sentence and think that it contains my assessment of what happened after Hitler attacked Poland — one man imposing his will on an entire people who couldn't help but be swept along. The problem is that the sentence could suggest a version of history that is monocausal, refusing to acknowledge a complex web of guilt and responsibility. I worry about being misunderstood in these pages, where I want to think about the kind of legacy World War II and, more specifically, the Holocaust have left for me, how their traces still shape the texture of my experience. I am used to choosing my words with care when I write, but with this topic the stakes are higher than on other occasions. The magnitude of what happened, its moral gravity, and the fact that I am German exert a rare kind of pressure on my language. Come to think of it, I wonder not only about the last sentence of the opening. It now occurs to me that I should reconsider the whole idea of starting with the movie, a somewhat quirky and distant opening that may call into question my willingness to address what is difficult.

Here is another beginning: A few years ago, while looking at some old photographs my mother keeps in a shoe box, I found a picture of my father. The picture was taken in the summer of 1944 and shows my father standing in a row of seven boys. Each boy has his arms wrapped around the shoulders of his neighbor, and most of them manage a tentative smile. Except for one, all of the boys are in uniform — black shorts, belt and buckle, brown shirt, and scarf. My father is twelve in this picture, and he is a member of the Deutsches Jungvolk, the lowest branch of the Hitler Youth. A red-and-white tassel stretches from his left shirt pocket across the scarf and identifies him as a Jungenschaftsführer, someone in charge of ten to fifteen other boys. When I asked my father about the picture, I learned that he had later been promoted to Jungzugführer, proudly exchanging his red-and-white tassel for a green one and accepting responsibility for some forty boys. He doesn't remember how he qualified for this promotion, but he must have done well in the serious games the Hitler Youth had thought up to supply the Reich with future soldiers — the parades, the night marches, the summer camps. At age twelve, my father belonged to the Deutsches Jungvolk with enthusiasm, and when the news of Claus Graf Schenk von Stauffenberg's assassination attempt on Hitler reached his summer camp in 1944, he and the other boys were distraught and angry, failing to understand why anyone would do such a thing. Two months after the war, my grandmother, afraid of the Russian soldiers patrolling the streets, threw my father's uniform into the manure pit behind their house.

She also threw away the uniform of my father's sister, Helga, who had belonged to the Jungmädel, the girls' version of the Deutsches Jungvolk. The normal age for joining the Jungmädel had been ten, but my aunt had begged my grandparents to let her join a year early, and they had finally given in. The first time I heard this detail, my surprise must have shown, because my aunt was suddenly eager to make me understand. "You see," she said, "what appealed to me so much was that it made me feel like an adult. I felt important and useful." As a Jungmädel my aunt performed "Snow-White and the Seven Dwarfs" in front of injured soldiers, and she prepared Christmas packages for troops at the front. She knitted gloves and ear-warmers, the task so important to her that she couldn't sleep at night, wondering whether her rest might endanger Germany's victory.

It is strange for me to think of my father and my aunt inside the perimeters of the Third Reich. I am startled by the ease with which their childhood world intersected with the rituals of Nazism, as if I half expected their moral compasses to have been fully developed, ready to dismiss what was threatening their humanity. But such an expectation pushes the need for moral scrutiny out of focus. It is my grandparents who belong at the center of this scrutiny, and it is the pattern of their lives that I find myself measuring against the need for accountability. I wonder, for example, why my father's parents, Albert and Frieda, gave in to Helga's desire to join the Jungmädel one year early. Even though the pressure to have children enter the various branches of the Hitler Youth was considerable and had in fact become law in 1936, I don't understand my grandparents' willingness to indulge their nine-year-old daughter's blind excitement. It seems to me that anyone who felt that the tenets of National Socialism were wrong should have been glad to keep their child out of reach of these tenets for as long as possible, especially if it involved no risk.

My instinct, as I try to reenvision the life that belonged to Albert and Frieda more than fifty years ago, is to look for consistency — a clear-cut position concerning the events of the day that would allow me to draw clear-cut conclusions. But what few details I know don't stack up so neatly. Albert served in the military twice, first in the Navy, and later as an infantryman outside of Hamburg. Near the end of the war, he was released from military service and sent back to work in the Hamburg shipyards, where his mechanical skills helped to build submarines. In the stories my father and his sister tell about Albert, who died in an accident in 1947, he is a man loyal to the Social Democrats, someone with little use for Nazi ideology. Not too long after the war began, one story goes, Albert and his two brothers, Walter and Kalli, beat up a storm trooper who had made the mistake of coming into their neighborhood pub in uniform. The three brothers bought the man drinks until he couldn't see straight, then dragged him outside and thrashed him. It was a rash and risky act that could have landed them in serious trouble, but, with Albert at least, such impulsive behavior seems to have been nothing unusual. As early as 1934 he had spent several days in prison for raising a ruckus when he felt treated unfairly by an insurance company. Insisting on a contractual technicality, the company had refused to pay the medical bills after Helga's birth, and my grandfather wasn't about to back down. Neither my father nor my aunt can recall what he did, but it was enough to get him arrested, sending Frieda into a string of worried, sleepless nights.

There is one story about Albert, something my father remembers in vague outlines, that holds my attention with particular insistence. The company my grandfather worked for in the Hamburg harbor, Blohm & Voß, used prisoners of war as cheap labor. From October 1944 until April 1945 the company also maintained a small work camp on its premises, which it filled with male inmates from the nearby Neuengamme concentration camp. According to my father, Albert at one point was caught trying to make contact with one of the prisoners, which led to a severe reprimand from his superiors. My father doesn't know whether Albert's transgression involved a prisoner of war or one of the camp inmates; he also doesn't know the exact nature of the transgression, whether Albert simply stopped to chat or whether he may have tried to share food and drink. It pleases me that Albert, at least in this one instance, seems to have ignored the rules to follow his own idea of right and wrong, and yet the pleasure I feel is thin and short-lived. Working close to concentration camp inmates, Albert must have caught glimpses of their angular bodies and faces. He was likely to hear stories and rumors about the destiny of these men, and this heightens my expectations for Albert; it makes me impatient for signs of more tangible and sustained resistance on the part of my grandfather.

If Albert had an impulsive streak that often got him into trouble, Frieda seems to have been eager to balance out her husband's spurts of unpredictability. My aunt Helga describes her mother as a strong, self-reliant woman who was fiercely protective of her family. Frieda died when I was six, but what few memories I have of her go well with the stories my aunt tells. I remember a tall, slender woman who moved with sparse elegance and whose eyes could read me like a book. Helga thinks that Frieda's concern for the family outweighed her concern for the political realities of the Third Reich, leading her to adopt a strategy of quiet adaptation — a pragmatic arrangement with the rules of the day to ensure her family's invisibility. One story, which illustrates my aunt's version of things, involves an oversize Nazi flag Frieda used to fly outside the window of their fourth floor apartment. At the time, German citizens were expected to own a flag and to fly it on official occasions, but my grandmother appears to have taken this request to an extreme. The flag she owned and flew was large enough to reach across two floors, billowing lazily under its own weight and making my grandfather groan with displeasure each time he saw it. It didn't matter to Frieda that her husband thought her silly. For her, my aunt believes, the flag was insurance against outside scrutiny, a way to fortify her family's realm of safety. When the war ended and my grandmother found her family in need of food and clothing, she took the flag and, in an act filled with its own kind of symbolism, turned it into a red and white dress for her daughter.

As with Albert and Frieda, the stories I have about my mother's parents are far from complete. In fact, I know even less about their wartime lives. They too passed away early, in my midteens, before my curiosity about our family's past had grown into questions. And unlike Helga, whose mind travels back in time easily, my mother isn't too interested in the cumbersome pace of memory work. But here is what I do know: My mother's father, Hans Kirchhoff, didn't serve in the military. Together with his father, Johann, and his brother, Erich, he ran the family business, a beer and beverage wholesale company that had been listed as essential to the war effort. What made the business essential, it seems, was the fact that it delivered part of its drinks to the cafeterias of local military industries, places where workers assembled anything from heavy engines to entire airplanes. While Hans spent his days at the company, his wife, Anni, stayed at home, neither one of them, according to my mother, political supporters of the National Socialists. No anecdotes or details exist to flesh out my mother's memory on this point, and I'm not sure how she has arrived at this perception of her parents' political views. What I do know is that my mother, who was born in 1934, belonged to the Jungmädel from 1944 until the end of the war.

There is also a photograph I should mention. This one I didn't find in a shoe box, and it doesn't show my mother or her parents. The picture, glued carefully into an album, is of my great-grandmother Anna, Johann's wife. It was taken during a trip to the coast, probably in the late thirties, and shows Anna sitting in a large covered wicker chair on the beach. Her face, relaxed and pleasant, is turned sideways toward the camera. She wears white pants, a white shirt, and a dark head scarf, most likely to protect her hair from the wind. Sand has been piled up in a circle around the wicker chair, and someone has taken the time to smooth out the surface of the sand and decorate it with shells. What captures my attention is a string of small, triangular flags stretching from the top of the chair down to the circle of sand, each flag displaying the crisp geometry of a swastika. I ask myself what these flags mean. Another picture in the album shows several seaplanes parked along what looks like the same beach. The planes too are marked with swastikas, and I have imagined that my great-grandmother or her husband picked up the flags, more or less by accident, at a Nazi rally that happened to descend upon their vacation village. But it is also possible, of course, that they brought the flags with them from Hamburg, planning all along to fly them at the beach. Whatever the details may be, what I wonder about more urgently is how far those flags reached into my great-grandparents' thoughts and actions.

The patchwork of stories I have about my family contains no examples of heroism, no courageous and purposeful resistance to the Nazi regime. It also lacks examples of blatant and violent evil. Instead, the stories add up to something in between, the familiar gray of questionable compromise or, as Karl Jaspers put it in 1946, "the commission of countless acts of negligence, of convenient adaptation, of cheap vindication, and the imperceptible promotion of wrong." The guilt in this case doesn't cluster around one or two significant acts, but it coats the patterns of everyday living like fine powder.

To enter my family's stories like this, assigning accountability, is a tricky journey for me. Not only am I aware that the stories I do know may be less significant than the stories I don't know, but I want to make sure that the clarity of hindsight, which I happen to enjoy, doesn't take away the complexity of the lives belonging to my grandparents and great-grandparents. For me, who has had the chance to scrutinize the Third Reich with the help of books, documentaries, and movies, the moral requirements of that period stand out like flagpoles, allowing virtually no competing focus. But what I try to remind myself of is the density of lived experience at any one moment in time, the layers of small acts and everyday occurrences — a friend calling to chat, a child coming down with chickenpox, a paycheck falling short of needs — all of which require attention and aren't void of moral substance and challenge. I try to recall such things not to deny the guilt that is present, but to find the right context for it and to prevent Albert, Frieda, Anna, and the others from becoming abstractions in a historical equation. What I also try to recall is the risk that any resistance to the regime did involve. Five decades removed from the events, I find it necessary to line my judgment with the awareness that my own moral stamina has yet to face a comparable test.

I have asked myself why the legacy of Word War II has become more relevant to me, how it is that this part of the past, now more than before, insists on finding a place in my present. Some of this, I'm sure, is the simple result of growing older. I am in my thirties now, and I no longer believe, as I may have done at eighteen, that the past and present are separate and that the latter is my private playing field. But there are also other things at work. Ever since November 9, 1989, when the Wall came down in Berlin, questions about Germany's future have surfaced in many places. What kind of country will a reunited Germany be? How will it settle into Europe? Is today's right-wing violence the sign of a shift in German ideology? These may be questions about the future, but they are built on the past. The difficult and untried process of reunification has turned German history into something tangible again, a force to be reckoned with outside the realm of academic debate.

On a more personal level, it matters that for eight out of the last ten years I have lived away from Germany. During this time I have studied and taught in America, living the life of a foreigner. And to be foreign in a place, in my experience, means to encounter oneself in the unfamiliar role of cultural representative. In many ways, my national identity has become visible to me only after I've had to measure it against other customs and the grainy perceptions of Germany that exist in America. Some of those perceptions I have found clichéd, others astute, but they all have led me to think about what, if anything, it means to be German. Naturally, World War II and the Holocaust figure among these perceptions, and so I have thought again about their significance from this side of the Atlantic, registering their echoes in conversations with friends, in newspapers, in museums, or even in the undigested symbolism of a horror movie.

During a recent visit with my family in Hamburg, on a Saturday in late June, I took a trip to the southeastern edge of the city. It took me forty minutes by car to reach the former site of the Neuengamme concentration camp. I had not taken this trip before. For several years in the late seventies, my family would drive past the site on the way to our weekend cottage, but we never took the final turn that would have landed us at the entrance to the memorial. This time I did turn and followed the curves of the two-lane road that took me past well-kept brick houses, many still built with thatched roofs. In this part of the city the houses begin to make room for fields, and a few times I had to slow down for tractors, their owners busy with the tasks of early summer. The closer I got to the former camp site, the more intensely I looked at the houses, the fields, and the handful of pedestrians. I wondered whether some of the older people I saw had already lived here in the forties, whether they had witnessed prisoners being taken to the camp. And part of me expected some change to occur in the landscape itself that could serve as a reminder of what had happened. But there was no such change — everything remained lush and full of life as I slowed down the car and made the final turn onto Jean-Dolidier-Weg.

The history of the Neuengamme camp begins in 1938. In December of that year, one hundred prisoners arrived from the concentration camp at Sachsenhausen to rebuild an old brick factory. For about eighteen months, Neuengamme served as an extension of Sachsenhausen before it became an independent camp in June 1940. One of the first things new prisoners saw as they entered the Neuengamme compound was the brutally cynical slogan painted in large letters onto the roof of the kitchen building: "There is a way to freedom. Its milestones are: obedience, diligence, honesty, order, cleanliness, abstinence, truthfulness, the ability to sacrifice, and love for the fatherland." Between 1938 and 1945, some 106,000 men and women from all over Europe were imprisoned in Neuengamme and its extension camps. About 55,000 of them died, many from sheer exhaustion as they labored in the brick factory or were forced to dig a massive canal to the nearby Elbe river. Others were killed by hanging, shooting, poison gas, or injection. During the first years of the camp, corpses were taken to the crematory at the Ohlsdorf cemetery some twenty-five kilometers to the north. After 1942, Neuengamme had its own crematory, and there is evidence that the SS staff used the ashes as fertilizer in the camp nursery and garden.

To get to the parking lot of the memorial, I had to drive to the end of Jean-Dolidier-Weg, past the entire length of the former camp. When the first buildings appeared on my left, I saw that one of them was a large concrete square, dotted with watchtowers and cameras, all of it — including a row of barred, slender windows — adding up to the look of a modern prison. A metal sign along the road warned passersby not to make contact with inmates, and it took me a few seconds to understand that the sign sent its message in the present and wasn't part of some historical display. I had known that the city operated a prison in this area, but until now had had no idea that it sat on top of the former camp site, still using some of the original buildings.

Later that day I would learn that the prison had started up only three years after the war and had triggered a wave of protest from former camp inmates. In 1951 they wrote a letter to Hamburg's mayor, Max Brauer, asking him to open at least part of the prison and grant visitors access to the site of the old camp crematory. The mayor ignored their request. "I believe," he wrote back, "that we should do our utmost through a mutual desire for understanding to reconcile the frightful atrocities of the past epoch as soon as possible and to gradually erase them from living memory." For Brauer, a "modern and humane prison" would serve as a "quiet memorial to the pitiable victims of the concentration camp." Some forty years later, in 1990, another Hamburg mayor, Henning Voscherau, had a very different take on the prison. "It was wrong," he wrote, "to establish the Vierlande prison on the grounds of the former concentration camp. . . . And if that was wrong, we should call it wrong — and at last move to change it. The Senate and this city will transfer the prison elsewhere and give the former concentration camp buildings back to the memorial center." The day I visited the memorial center, seven years after Voscherau's promise, I detected no signs of an imminent move. The prison appeared solid and operational, some of the inmates milling about on what looked like a fenced-in soccer field. I had to walk along a stretch of the prison fence after I had parked my car, and I remember studying its sleek metal skeleton with a feeling of profound embarrassment.

But this embarrassment, triggered by the fence and the historical and moral amnesia it stood for, was only part of what I experienced as I followed the gravel path into the memorial. Most of all, I noticed a rush of competing thoughts and emotions, an internal overload that felt familiar. I had felt the same on my one previous visit to a concentration camp — Buchenwald outside Weimar. And I had also felt it a year earlier as I had studied the displays at the Holocaust Memorial Museum in Washington, D.C. It is a confusion triggered by the awareness that the place I have come to requires a reaction from me and not knowing what that reaction should be. One part of me enters such a place ready to analyze, eager to understand the causal links that added up to the Holocaust. I feel free to question, compare, speculate, knowing that only such scrutiny can help clarify how the events came about and who was responsible. But another part of me feels that such a rational approach, while well-intentioned, misses the point. This part pulls me away from language, narrative, and purposeful inquiry, leaving me silent in the face of suffering. This part doesn't visit the former camp with a desire to learn but with a desire to honor the memory of the victims. And as I slide back and forth between these two frames of mind, my body too gets pulled into uncertainty. As someone who comes to learn and inquire, I am at ease in my body and move around at whatever pace I find comfortable. I might yawn when I begin to feel tired, or I might take a bottle of water out of my backpack and quench my thirst. But as someone who comes to honor the memory of the dead, I don't feel the same ease. Then, my visit takes on the significance of ritual, and I feel the need to let my body express that reality. I slow it down and move with care. I am reluctant to disturb the spiritual content of the place I have come to.

In a book about the memories of war in Germany and Japan, Ian Buruma writes that "you can remember the Holocaust through art, through ceremony, or through analysis and disclosure, but you cannot do all this at the same time, or in the same place." I find this to be true, and yet as I entered the Neuengamme site I again found myself suspended between ceremony and analysis, not knowing which instinct to follow or trust. Even inside the exhibit that documents the camp history, I felt the same ambiguity. The exhibit, which is housed in one of the original camp buildings, is well-done. Most of the displays are supported by long metal rods, welded together at odd angles. The rods are the kind that gets used in construction, and they give the exhibit an industrial feel — a reminder of the camp's murderous ties to business. Between the rods, the displays seem almost delicate, whispering rather than shouting, pulling the visitor into private dialogue. Some of the displays are hidden inside drawers, and one has to open them to take a look. The first drawer I opened contained a piece of old cloth with a prisoner's number. Another revealed a yellowed notebook listing daily food rations. With each drawer I opened, my sense of ambiguity came back, one part of me a student looking for information, forgetful of my own movements, the other part a visitor paying respect, aware of my arm reaching out, the weight of the drawer, the texture of wood against my fingertips.

After I left the exhibit, I followed the walkway through the memorial. I passed by the canal prisoners had dug to the Elbe river. A slight breeze rippled the brackish water, and a handful of seagulls tumbled through the air above it. Then I came to the abandoned brick factory, a massive structure, which now faces a five-meter-high wall and a watchtower belonging to the Vierlande prison. Some of the trolleys camp prisoners had used to transport raw clay to the factory still stood in their tracks nearby. The large trolleys had long since begun to rust, and pools of rainwater had collected inside them. Still it was easy to tell how hard it must have been to push the loaded trolleys even under the best of conditions, not to mention exhausted from hunger and torture. As I stood in front of the brick factory, one of the prison guards stared at me from the watchtower, but when I looked up to make eye contact he turned away.

Near the end of the walkway, I stopped at the former camp train station. A group of high school students and their teacher had arrived before me, standing in a circle around their guide, listening as she explained how the trains had found their way to Neuengamme. The students looked to be around fifteen or sixteen years old, dressed casually, some of them disappearing in oversize jeans, almost all of them wearing sneakers. The teacher was a short man in his forties whose attention kept shifting back and forth between the guide and the group in his charge. There wasn't much left of the train station. No buildings or platforms, just a single wooden boxcar on a set of grass-covered tracks. The door of the boxcar was open, and the open frame had been filled with a painting of prisoners standing huddled together. "Some of the trains arriving in Neuengamme brought up to two thousand prisoners," the guide said. "Usually each boxcar carried about a hundred prisoners, who often had to endure journeys of two to three days without stops or relief of any kind." The teacher let his eyes travel around the circle of students but found nothing to worry about. Most of them were paying attention.

Right in front of the boxcar, a cement rectangle stretched across the ground, and now the guide asked the students to study it more closely. I did the same. The rectangle was covered with pairs of footprints, one hundred of them, and the size of the rectangle was the size of the boxcar. It was a simple but effective way of showing how crowded the cars had been. As soon as the guide had finished her explanation, the students began to move onto the rectangle, slowly, taking small steps, choosing a pair of footprints, then sliding their sneakers into the shallow indentations. The guide kept talking, outlining the brutal initiation into camp life that awaited prisoners after they had been unloaded. She described the hours newcomers had to stand at attention outdoors, even in the midst of winter. She mentioned the surrender of all personal belongings and the rushed, frantic showers. She talked about the thirty or so barbers who shaved off the prisoners' hair, all of it, handling the bodies like pieces of wood. It was during this part of the guide's presentation that one of the students groaned. We all turned around to look because we could tell the note of genuine horror in the sound, and its unguardedness took us by surprise. The student, a girl dressed in a jean jacket with shoulder-length red hair, still stood in a pair of footprints on the cement rectangle. She seemed embarrassed by her own show of emotion and wasn't sure where to look. "They did what?" she finally managed to say. It was clear that she didn't need anything repeated. She wanted us to turn away, and we did, waiting for the guide to go on.

When I climbed into my car half an hour later, I was still thinking about what had happened on the cement rectangle. I could see the students shuffling into the footprints, and I could hear the sound of the girl's voice. But the more I thought about what I had witnessed, the more complicated the scene at the former camp train station became. My first reaction was positive. The students' response struck me as a good example of how the Neuengamme memorial should work, bridging the gap between past and present. For a moment, the students seemed to have fallen out of the routine of a school excursion and into a fuller understanding of the suffering that had taken place. And yet there was something about this moment of connection that remained questionable. How appropriate was it in the end for a group of German students to identify with the victims of the Holocaust? Wasn't this kind of emotional investment misplaced, allowing an easy and disingenuous catharsis? I wondered about this not just because of the students, but also because of myself. I too had felt my imagination move inside the boxcar and then through the brutal stages of the camp initiation. In front of the brick factory, I had put my hands on one of the trolleys and tried to move it. Standing next to the canal, I had filled the space on my left and right with uniformed prisoners, exhausted men holding on to shovels and wheelbarrows.

I have learned that it is tempting to give in to the imagination in places like Neuengamme. The students must have noticed this as well, and I wonder whether their teacher discussed their reaction after they had all returned to the classroom. What is difficult, I think, is to find the right balance in all of this. It is presumptuous to believe that any act of the imagination can contain the suffering that took place. And even if I think of the imagination as something more partial, a rough approximation, I have to be on guard against its sentimental pull that slides me into the role of victim. My obligation to be on guard has to do with the simple fact that I am German, a citizen of the country in which the Holocaust happened. For me, the Neuengamme memorial has to tell two stories — the story of the victims and the story of the perpetrators, men and women who belong to the history of my home and whose actions have shaped my identity. It is their legacy I have to study as objectively as I can and then let influence the scope of my thoughts and actions. But, as Buruma emphasizes, there is, of course, still room for the imagination. To approach the past without it — either on the side of the victims or the perpetrators — would be to flatten the past, to take away some of its complexity and moral relevance.

In the end, Neuengamme, and places like it, will continue to be complicated territory for me. I arrive in them as a student, a mourner, and as a German, my frame of reference never quite at rest. I don't know what constitutes the right kind of reaction, and I doubt there is one. But I do know that I have to come to these places willing to let their different dimensions move through me, resisting the impulse to simplify what lacks simplicity.

Not too long ago, in America, I signed up for a two-week writing class. The teacher, a woman from Utah, had much to say about writers as members of a community who depend on each other's efforts and ideas. To make this point once more on the last day of class, she had the students read their final essays in random order, without interruption, leaving it up to us to decide when to jump in and be heard. It was a new setup for most of us, and I kept wondering when I should volunteer my few pages. I didn't want to read too early for fear of seeming overly eager, and I also didn't want to read at the end, as if holding out for the final spotlight. I decided to read somewhere in the middle, but when the slot I had chosen arrived, I didn't take it. The reason for my silence at that moment had nothing to do with being nervous. I didn't read because Dorian, the woman who had just finished, had shared a story that made me think. She had written about her family's escape from the Warsaw Ghetto, how they had spent months before in secret preparation, how they had climbed the ghetto wall at night and had begun life outside, pretending to be Catholics for three exhausting years. She wrote about her own trip to Poland together with her grandfather. She wrote about their visit to the house that had once been her family's hiding place. She wrote about the desire to attach the stories she had heard all her life to actual places. It was a beautiful piece, and when she had finished I knew I wouldn't read next.

My reason for keeping silent in that moment didn't have anything to do with the subject of my own short essay. There was nothing in my piece that connected it to German history, nothing that could have come across as a provocation. In fact, I had written about something perfectly unrelated — how, years ago, I had made a fool of myself while working as a field hand in California. My reason for not reading was this: Like most students in the class, Dorian knew I was German, and I didn't want her to think, even briefly, that her story didn't matter to me, that I could rush right by it with the noise of my own words. I realize that my reaction may have been unnecessary. It is possible, maybe even likely, that neither Dorian nor any of the other students would have thought twice about my story following hers. And yet, in the few minutes I had to decide whether to read or not, as I tried to measure the distance between the past and the present, I grew reluctant to let my story be the one to push ahead.

A few weeks after the class had ended, when Dorian and I had discovered that we both tried to understand legacies of the Holocaust in our writing, we decided to exchange drafts of our work. We set up a meeting in the café of a local bookstore, and I remember being unsure about how we would be able to talk to each other. On the appointed day she arrived at the café before I did, waiting at a table next to the coffee counter, studying her notes. The first thing I noticed after we had said hello was her necklace. It was a heavy silver chain linked to a silver plate. The design on the plate resembled an open eye with the word *courage* engraved below it. Throughout our conversation I looked at the necklace from time to time, and I wondered whether its message had helped to fortify its owner to come here today and talk. I told Dorian what I had found out so far about my family's lives during the Third Reich, and she listened intently. She was relieved when none of the stories I touched on put my family in the center of what had happened, revealed direct ties to the National Socialists or the crimes committed. "I'm not sure I could have sat here and talked with you otherwise," she said, and I was surprised again, not by her reaction, but by how close the past does travel to the present. We spoke about our shared sense that to write about one's connection to the Holocaust can feel presumptuous and inevitable at the same time. We spoke about the difficulty of pitching stories toward an event that, at its core, seems to negate story. And when we had lost some of our nervousness, we turned to the drafts we had brought and began to discuss the flow of ideas, the shape of paragraphs, the odd angle of a metaphor. In all we sat for about an hour in that bookstore café, not much time really, but after we said good-bye, Dorian staying at the table to do some more reading and I making my way to the door, our meeting began to feel to me like a chance well-used, a chance to grant each other room inside an intricate history.

I am aware that this meeting at a bookstore somewhere in Iowa, no matter from what angle one may look at it, is a small event. But over time I have come to realize that much of the challenge of engaging the legacy of the Holocaust, at least for me, resides in the realm of the small, and not in some large design that can somehow echo the magnitude of Auschwitz. The spaces of my days are too narrow for such an ambition. Instead, I'm left with a string of moments in which I can choose to be awake to this part of the past, allowing it to have a say in how I draw the boundary between myself and what surrounds me. A fellow student across the table. A place of memory on the outskirts of my city. A picture of my great-grandmother on a wind-blown beach. A sentence of my own making. There is still plenty of room for mistakes, even in the realm of the small, for drawing the boundary in the wrong place. But the point, it seems to me, is to keep trying to get it right, to anchor my self inside of motion as the past washes into my present, and thus to make the past, carefully and imperfectly, an instrument of my humanity.

Language Lessons

Dr. Ward had a hard time with German. In fact, he spoke only a handful of words. He could say "Guten Tag" and "Auf Wiedersehen," and when he sat in a restaurant, he knew when to use "bitte" and "danke." He also picked up the expression "ach so," which means something like "oh really" or "I get it," depending on a speaker's intonation. Whenever Dr. Ward used "ach so," he slaughtered the words. All of their softness disappeared, and he sounded like an angry Japanese samurai ready to strike. I told him so, and he liked the comparison. He started using the expression more often after that, studying my reaction, waiting for me to smile. Technically, Dr. Ward should have been able to speak some German, to have what the diplomatic corps calls "courtesy level" fluency. But somehow he had managed to get assigned to Berlin without fulfilling this basic requirement. As the Regional English Teaching Officer for eastern Germany, the Czech Republic, and Slovakia, he would work mostly with local English teachers, people who had learned to speak his language, and so he saw no real need to do battle with foreign syntax.

I started working for Dr. Ward late in 1991. My official job title was Cultural Affairs Specialist, which mostly meant that I was Dr. Ward's secretary, responsible for everything from copying handouts to preparing quarterly budget plans. I was also a Foreign Service National, a German working for the United States Information Agency (USIA) in Germany. A friend of mine had seen the job ad in one of the Berlin papers and had given me a call in Hamburg, where I was shuffling résumés and cover letters, waiting for an opportunity to come along. Just two months earlier, I had returned from the United States. I had been working on a doctorate in English, but after three years of graduate school the rituals of reading and writing had begun to feel thin and distant. I wasn't sure what was at stake anymore. For the most part, the words I read and wrote felt uninspired, ready to bend into whatever version of reality came in the most handy. It didn't help that I saw the Wall come down on a small black-and-white TV set in my study; my country reuniting next to a stack of nineteenth-century American novels. I watched people embrace in the streets of Berlin. I saw their faces flushed with joy. And gradually, the images began to tug at my attention. I wanted to understand what was happening at home, and in the end I packed my books into twelve boxes and left them in a friend's attic.

My interview with Dr. Ward took place in what had been the American embassy in the old East Berlin — an imposing turn-of-the-century structure, not far from the Brandenburg Gate. After I had walked through the metal detector and received a visitor's pass, I waited for Dr. Ward in the lobby. He showed up a few minutes late, a small man in a gray suit who greeted me in a high, enthusiastic voice. "How are you?" he said, and ushered me into another room, an abandoned library full of empty shelves. Near the back of the library, a small office opened up on the right, and this was the place Dr. Ward had chosen for our interview. We sat down across from each other, but right away Dr. Ward got up again. "It's dark in here, isn't it?" he said. "I wonder where the light switch might be." He began to walk along the walls, looking. I wasn't sure what to do. I was nervous, eager to make a good impression. And then it occurred to me that this was all part of the interview. Dr. Ward knew where the light switch was. He wanted to see whether I would get up and help him, whether I'd be the kind of man who would roll up his sleeves and pitch in. We searched for about five minutes, and I tried to look efficient and purposeful. A couple of times I even spoke out loud, letting Dr. Ward in on my reasoning why one part of the room promised more success than another. We never found the switch. Instead, we sat down again and began the interview, a bit of daylight falling on the desk between us.

Dr. Ward called me in Hamburg the next day and offered me the job, and I accepted. I was looking forward to working in the five new German states. Except for a weeklong high school trip, I had never visited the German Democratic Republic. It had been another country — remote, forbidding, of no consequence to the life I imagined for myself. But before I could start working, I had to get an apartment in

Berlin. Everyone I spoke to thought it might take six months or more to find a place. Since the Wall had come down, the city was overrun with newcomers, all of them looking for affordable housing. Somehow I got lucky. After three days of studying newspapers and making phone calls, I signed a lease for an efficiency on the western edge of Charlottenburg. It was tiny and pricey, but not far from the lakes and woods of the Grunewald. I also went out and tried to do something about my wardrobe. My graduate school outfits clearly wouldn't do for a Cultural Affairs Specialist, a government employee in the field of public diplomacy. I bought a jacket, some slacks, a handful of ties, and, reluctantly, a dark gray, double-breasted suit. Then the only thing left to worry about was the security check.

As part of the application process, I had agreed to have my background looked over. I had signed a release of information, which authorized the State Department to check my biographical data, anything they might be interested in from education to former jobs. It was routine procedure, but it was new to me. One of the jobs I had listed was with our family business, a beer and beverage wholesale company where I had helped out over the years. A couple of weeks after I finished the paperwork, a letter arrived at my father's office. It was short and courteous, asking for confirmation of my data. The letter also asked, if possible, for an honest assessment of my character and my general aptitude for government work. My father, who has never been at ease around words, didn't want to write back. "You deal with this," he said, "and when you're done, I'll sign it." I debated for two days how to put together my letter of recommendation. In the end, I kept it short, just four sentences, two about the data I had given, two about my character and aptitude. I figured this was no time for rhetorical flourishes. After running through a list of adjectives that, more or less, fell into the ballpark of my potential, I settled on describing myself as "reliable" and "conscientious." And to make sure I didn't sound too staid even for government work, I threw in "flexible" and "sociable." I showed the letter to my father, who signed it without comment. Three weeks later I joined Dr. Ward in Berlin.

Our base of operations was the Amerika Haus, a U.S. cultural center built in the 1950s and located in the heart of the former West Berlin. The building was a string of three adjoining boxes, decorated above the entrance with a large, stylized American flag. Its architecture had the stale charm that comes from celebrating an old version of the future. Dr. Ward and I occupied two offices on the second floor, and as soon as we had settled in I began working the phones, calling universities all over eastern Germany to set up meetings. Our mission was to assist local English departments in their efforts to teach language classes. English language teaching had been an odd occupation under the old Socialist regime, something to be tolerated rather than encouraged. To know English might have been useful, even necessary, but it had also meant getting acquainted with a world beyond East German borders, a world caught up in the false promises of capitalism. Such an encounter could trigger confusion. It might hurt the formation of true Socialist personalities, and so was a risk best kept in check. But now, with the Wall gone, things were different. The old teaching materials would no longer do. It was time to catch up with the West, new methodologies and new research, and Dr. Ward and I were supposed to help. We had plans for putting together a video library and a professional newsletter. We had stacks of USIA publications to hand out. We would organize conferences, give out scholarships, bring in American lecturers. We would even set up roundtable discussions via satellite.

But before we could do any of these things, I was stuck on the phone. I had looked up the numbers of all eastern German universities and tried to dial my way down the list. Impossible. Most of the time I got busy signals, but even the calls that went through usually collapsed within the first minute. "Guten Tag, this is the Regional English Teaching Office. My name is" *click*. What Dr. Ward and I had failed to take into account was the simple fact that eastern Germany still had no comprehensive phone system. Day after day, work crews were out putting in new phone lines and repairing old ones. I had seen some of them at work in the eastern half of the city. They looked like surgeons wrestling oversize veins, slipping them underground in the hope to jump-start a giant. All I could do was be patient and keep dialing. Once in a while, after I had finished pressing the numbers, there would be nothing but a scratching sound, telling me that my electronic signal had gotten lost, taking wrong turns somewhere in Thuringia or Brandenburg. Then, after thirty seconds or so, a phone would ring, any phone. "Hello, Bauer Cement Company. Can I help you?"

While I was still trying to contact the universities, Dr. Ward learned about an independent language institute about an hour outside Berlin. He didn't know for sure what kind of institute it was, but he thought it was worth a visit, a chance to spread the news of our existence and make some contacts. I agreed, glad for any reason that would get me away from the phones. Our drive took us over narrow country roads, many of them lined with linden trees. It had snowed the night before, and the stillness of the powdered villages and fields felt like a surprise after the city's frantic pace. I followed our route on the map, while Dr. Ward maneuvered the Opel station wagon that belonged to the office. He had told me that the institute was housed in an eighteenth-century manor, a palace really, but I hadn't decided yet whether to believe him. It sounded a touch too grand for a language institute, and there was always the chance that Dr. Ward had misunderstood, trying his hand at translating German.

But he was right. The institute was a palace, and we couldn't have missed it, even if we had tried. It was an elegant, red-brick structure with countless gables and windows the size of ponds. Three or four other brick buildings sat right next to it, and beyond them stretched an impressive park full of ancient trees, bordered by a small, winding river. It looked unreal.

"Willkommen in Plaue!" Professor Kohls, the director of the institute, greeted us from behind his desk. He was around sixty, a man of medium height, barrel-chested, dressed in a slightly shabby blue jacket and a silk scarf that filled the open triangle of his shirt. He wore a pair of heavy, horn-rimmed glasses, and his gray hair had managed to grow an inch or so past his collar. The office we shook hands in was small, but every piece of furniture looked brand-new, as if it had been delivered just hours before. It was the kind of office furniture I had seen hundreds of times in western Germany, efficient and functional, designed in harmless beige. After we had sat down, Professor Kohls began by telling us about the history of his institute and the languages that were still taught here. He spoke in German, his sentences full of ornate turns and surprising vistas, and yet somehow unsure of their destination. While he talked, he uneasily sat in his new office chair, as if hiding behind someone else's desk, worried about getting caught. "Why don't I show you around a bit," he concluded after a few more sentences. "That way, you'll get a much better idea." I translated for Dr. Ward, and we followed the director out into the hall.

Professor Kohls led us through long hallways with linoleum floors, up and down stairs sandpapered by thousands of shoes. He took us past tall windows framed by bright orange curtains, past scattered groups of chairs, and Formica tables pushed against walls. Outside the small office, the institute stood still, quietly reclaiming the texture of an earlier decade. Walking us through his familiar terrain, Professor Kohls seemed to gain some assurance, and even the old-fashioned flamboyance of his scarf began to look inspired. "We believe language teaching must take place in a relaxed atmosphere," he said, pointing to a few chairs in front of a television set. "Have a seat. I want to show you a short film about what we do here." Dr. Ward and I sat down, and the film began to roll, taking us on another tour through the institute, showing us the same rooms, only this time they weren't empty.

In one scene, a group of East German men and women recited English sentences in what looked like a living room. There were armchairs and well-watered plants, beautiful oriental carpets and bookshelves. Every once in a while the teacher would ask the students to get up and walk around, which they did with careful, hypnotic steps. At other times, the students had to lean back in their chairs and close their eyes. Classical music would start up and waft through the room for several minutes. Then, it was back to reciting. I had never seen anything like it. Dr. Ward, however, seemed to know the approach. He chuckled and shook his head. The film switched from classroom to living quarters: Dressed in pajamas, two middle-aged men crawled under their covers and reached up to two bulky headsets wired into the wall. They put on the headsets and fell back onto their pillows, eyes closed, listening. The lesson continued as they drifted off into sleep, foreign words skirting the edge of their dreams. Dr. Ward chuckled again.

I had thought that Professor Kohls might leave us alone in front of the TV. He must have known the film by heart. But he sat right next to us, watching as intently as we did. Earlier in his office, he had worried about the growing indifference of local officials toward the institute; he knew that a language school dealing in matters of the subconscious would have a hard time surviving the solid sweep of reunification. When the film ended, he invited us to lunch in the cafeteria. We were the only ones eating, and the clatter of our forks and knives echoed through the dining hall. I expected Professor Kohls to propose future projects, ways we might work together, but he remained silent. He seemed distracted and distant. We said good-bye outside his office, promising to be in touch. As soon as we had pulled out of the courtyard, Dr. Ward looked over at me. "What a trip. Can you believe that place?" I nodded. But what I thought about in that moment were the two men falling asleep with their headsets on. I wondered what language they had been listening to that night, years before reunification. Had they expected to travel outside East Germany? Maybe they had belonged to the privileged few who could, maybe not. And if they hadn't, then those words trickling through their headsets must have carried real weight, filled with the promise of other countries. Maybe that was the true virtue of Professor Kohl's approach—for moments at a time, inside the unlikely atmosphere of a brick palace, he had turned words into places.

We never returned to Plaue. Back in Berlin, I wrote a brief follow-up letter to the institute, and once I tried to get through on the phone, but the line wouldn't hold.

It took me two weeks to finish calling the universities on my list. I usually spent the mornings on the phone and kept the afternoons free for other projects. For several days, I read some of the old East German textbooks, with titles like *English for You* or *Modern English*. I was curious about their approach. One of the volumes was structured around the U.S. visit of a Soviet journalist, who had the uncanny ability to run into American social problems. After his arrival in Washington, he rents a taxi for a quick sightseeing tour, and his driver, a young black man from Alabama (who has been mugged three times but still sends money home), comes right to the point. "The laws made by Congress are not for the people but for Big Business," he tells his international passenger as they glide past the Capitol. In New York, the friendly Pan Am tour guide, Jim Edwards, takes the journalist through Harlem. Jim is well-prepared and has the statistics about tuberculosis, unemployment, and infant death at his fingertips. Undaunted by this urban nightmare, the Soviet journalist gets on the transcontinental bus to Los Angeles. He has time to admire the reclining seats and the air-conditioning, but things soon turn glum again. Outside Salt Lake City, waking from slumber, he remembers labor organizer Joe Hill, who was executed by western copper bosses in 1915. He looks out across the Great Salt Lake Desert. Melancholy seizes him. He cannot help but think about all the other brave Americans who fought for a better future but ended up dead like Joe Hill.

They were all like that. No matter what the story idea, it was airtight. There were no loose ends. Reality was a perfect illustration of Marxist-Leninist theory. America and England had some charming corners, but they were still heading in the wrong direction, torn by class struggle and the blind pursuit of profit. But there was hope. Between pointers on passive voice and adverbs, students heard about the struggle of English labor unions and the tireless efforts of the American Communist party, which one day would make a difference. For the most part I found the books funny. They seemed like satires of themselves, ridiculous in their didactic passion. I had to agree that some of their criticism was well-taken, but all of it deflated when I compared it to what had really happened in East Germany, a dictatorship that had needed a wall to keep from bleeding dry. There was something claustrophobic and bloodless about the books. And yet, reading several in a row, I noticed that it was possible to give in to them. The sureness and symmetry with which they pinned down right and wrong became intoxicating, a broad current whose pull was difficult to resist.

Our own teaching materials kept arriving from Washington in a steady stream of packages. Since the shipments were usually heavy, we didn't bother carrying them up to our offices. We found an empty basement room and simply dumped the packages through its two narrow window slots. After every other shipment or so, I would spend a few hours opening the boxes and stacking their contents in piles. Some of the texts were straightforward grammar guides; others were simplified novels or short stories. There were streamlined versions of Twain's *The Adventures of Huckleberry Finn* and *Six Tales of Fear* by Edgar Allan Poe. The rest were mostly texts meant to serve as introductions to American society and customs. In one stack I kept *Celebrate! Holidays in the U.S.A*, in another *Crown of Eagles: The Life Stories of Ten Famous American Indians*, and in yet another *Basic Readings in U.S. Democracy*. We also had three different folders of miniposters that teachers could use to decorate their classrooms. The posters showed national landmarks like Hoover Dam or the Golden Gate Bridge, and also, again and again, wide-angle shots of blazing landscapes — lakes, mountains, deserts that sparkled in ambitious yellows and blues. Several of these shots had a line of poetry or prose floating in the sky, something profound to help focus the mood. One of the lines was by Thoreau and hung in the sundown above Arches National Monument: "Eastward I go by force, but westward I walk free." I didn't expect that poster to find many takers.

Dr. Ward and I weren't the only ones preparing for visits to the universities. The British Council had its headquarters next door to the Amerika Haus, and we knew they were trying to call the same numbers we did. One of their staff members, Dr. Frankl, was an old acquaintance of Dr. Ward's. They had met on a previous assignment, and they couldn't stand each other. Sometimes we ran into Dr. Frankl at a nearby cafeteria, where the conversation usually turned into a polite exchange of disinterest, spiced up here and there with touches of sarcasm. It was easy to see that Dr. Frankl thought of his American counterpart as a buffoon, a man who shouldn't belong to the diplomatic corps, that select group of men and women versed in languages, history, and good restaurants. In return, Dr. Ward thought of his British colleague as a snob, someone too pompous to ever be effective. He also took a certain joy in confirming Dr. Frankl's idea of him. He turned up the volume of his laughter and ordered dishes by pointing at the menu and saying, "Yum, yum," all the while rubbing his stomach in anticipation.

Whatever had started the dislike between Dr. Ward and Dr. Frankl, they now had an official reason to keep it alive. They both had been assigned to eastern Germany as language teaching officers, and they both knew that language wasn't all they were meant to trade. As public diplomats, they had to worry about building spheres of influence that should, at some point, bring economic and financial payoff. And neither one was thrilled about the competition. Seeing them taunt each other in the cafeteria, I sometimes thought of them as two developers eager to slice up a prime piece of beachfront property. In those moments, I was surprised to find myself at the same table, as if all three of us watched eastern Germany from the same dispassionate distance. For me, the places I contacted day after day were now part of the country I called my own, and that switch in perspective still startled me. I had put up a map of the five new German states in my office, each state a different color to help the eye make sense of what it saw. I studied the map and tried to commit it to memory. Gradually, I was beginning to get an idea of the cities and the distances between them. But none of that made it feel more real.

One of our first official visits took us to Potsdam University on the outskirts of Berlin. We arrived in gray suits, lugging a large box of USIA publications and a stack of handouts. The English department faculty was waiting in one of the conference rooms, where our contact, Dr. Klemm, introduced us to her colleagues. She was a thin, boyish woman, who spoke English with an impeccable British accent. I was surprised to hear the words come out with such nativelike precision. I didn't know yet that some British lecturers had taught summer courses in East Germany, and that a few of them had stayed on for good, mostly the ones who believed in the Socialist experiment. I also didn't know that many of the teachers had made good use of the radio, listening secretly to BFBS, the British Forces in West Berlin. They had tuned in the programs in the privacy of their homes and then studied the crisp flourish of the announcers and the chatter of the DJs like students scanning a pronunciation chart.

I had little to do during Dr. Ward's presentation. He spoke about our office and its goals, and once in a while I passed around a handout to illustrate the points he was making. Dr. Ward began to warm to his subject, outlining the great opportunities he saw for future cooperation and projects. He took off his jacket and darted back and forth, his blue tie swinging like a pendulum between red suspenders. He brought up the video library we were putting together and the plans we had for a professional newsletter. He mentioned the English teaching fellows we would fly over and, after a short but meaningful pause, the opportunity for satellite links.

Despite his obvious enthusiasm, the room stayed lukewarm. Most of the teachers seemed to pay attention, but it looked as if they had to make a conscious effort, as if something else were working in the back of their minds. One of the teachers, an older man sitting across from me, kept his eyes fixed on the notepad in front of him. He didn't write anything down, his hands stayed locked in a tight ball. He gave no sign that he was listening. The only time he lifted his eyes, he let them travel across the faces of his colleagues like someone double-checking an unlikely image.

It wasn't difficult to understand why the presentation didn't take off, why it floated above the audience, rarely triggering a question. The papers I read at the office every day were full of articles about the restructuring of eastern German universities — a vast project that would cost a lot of teachers their jobs. And some of those teachers were sitting at the table in this conference room, only nobody knew yet who they would be. It depended on how they would fare in front of the committees set up to judge their professional skills, and also their political loyalties. Anyone who had cooperated with the State Security Police, who had spied on colleagues and friends, would almost certainly have to go. But even if such clear-cut proof were missing, if the political committee came up with nothing, there was still the possibility of having one's competence called into question. Maybe one wouldn't have enough publications. Maybe they would be the wrong kind. Maybe the foreign language skills wouldn't suffice, now that the borders were open and everyone expected all language teachers to sound like a native.

Dr. Ward had opened the box of books we had brought and began to hold up a few of the titles, explaining how they might be worked into a successful syllabus. The older man across from me still stared at his notepad. I wondered whether he might already have heard about his chances to stay on. For all I knew, he could be facing the loss of his job in a week or two, asking himself what he was doing at this meeting. At his age, he would have a hard time finding other work. The longer he stared at his notepad, the more I believed I had figured out what worried him: He had lost his job. Day after day, there was more change. He found it hard to drive to work, to make it through traffic heavy with western cars. He lived in an old, spacious apartment whose newly adjusted rent was out of the question. In his neighborhood, houses disappeared under scaffolding to emerge again a few months later, new and sleek, filled with different faces. The bakery at the corner had closed down and made room for a computer store. Sometimes he stood in front of the display window and studied the keyboards and monitors, and even though he knew what he was looking at, the sight of those machines didn't want to make sense.

Dr. Ward was still busy with the books. I tried to concentrate on what he was saying, but couldn't for very long. What if my guesses about the teacher weren't that far off? It hadn't occurred to me until now that I might have misread the eyes fixed on the notepad, the clasped hands. I had seen resignation in those gestures, but now it seemed entirely possible that they contained rage. It also seemed possible that I was sitting somewhere inside that rage, one more face promising change. I sat up straight and fingered my tie. If the teacher looked up, I didn't want to appear indifferent or bored. And, of course, I wasn't. How could I be in this room full of men and women whose lives now cut across mine with such intimacy? I was curious. I wanted to understand something about their lives, not just their professional concerns. I wanted a hint whether all of our stories would fit together after forty years. Dr. Ward held up *A Crown of Eagles* followed by *From Sea to Shining Sea*, one of the folders with miniposters. I stirred in my chair, coughed, half hoping the sound would get the older teacher to look over. I'm not sure what I would have done if he had.

When the presentation ended, there was some polite applause and knocking on tables. Dr. Ward thanked everyone for coming, and Dr. Klemm thanked us in return. She seemed pleased with what she had heard, excited even. Unlike many of her colleagues, she was full of energy. I tried to gauge whether that energy was real or maybe just a cover for keeping her worries at bay. I couldn't tell. After the meeting, Dr. Klemm explained to us how to get to the other part of Potsdam campus, a few kilometers away, where we had scheduled another presentation for the afternoon. She was eager to have us memorize the details of the route. There were some unexpected turns, and she didn't want us to get lost.

The afternoon group was smaller, about ten teachers who taught English for special purposes. They were a kind of branch department responsible for working with law students and engineers. Our presentation was different too. We started out with the brief introduction to our office, but then Dr. Ward gave an actual lecture. The topic he had picked was "Techniques for Teaching Oral Skills." Instead of talking about the techniques in theory, he brought in several classroom exercises and planned to have the teachers play along like students. I had worried that this kind of approach might fall flat and be taken as condescending. But Dr. Ward didn't agree.

He began by grouping the teachers in pairs and then handed out cardboard sheets on which he had pasted Blondie cartoons. There were two kinds of sheets, labeled *A* and *B*, which had some cartoons in common and some that were subtly different. The teachers' task was to ask each other questions about the cartoons and to determine whether they were the same or not. When the sheets had gone around, Dr. Ward took off his jacket and stood up. "All ready?" he asked. Then he stretched out his arms in front of him, a foot apart, hands facing each other. A second later, he slapped his hands together and yelled "action" at the top of his lungs. The room was stunned into silence, which, slowly, turned into a wave of giggles. The exercise worked well. Soon the teachers were shooting questions back and forth and kidding each other about their wrong guesses. They asked Dr. Ward for help with words they didn't know, and he was good at helping them, quick and friendly, never surprised by their requests. He put them at ease, and I thought this had to do with his willingness to make himself vulnerable, to forget about diplomacy and teach with all the tricks of the trade—the chalk flying across the blackboard, the jokes, the right-sized questions, the careful listening. He continued to pull out more exercises, and the teachers continued to play along, recognizing their own teacherly ways in Dr. Ward's approach.

One of the last exercises was called "The Time Line." It was a simple setup: Students had to mark the major events of their lives on a time line and then create a story around the choices they had made. A woman near the front of the room volunteered. She looked to be in her forties, her pale face framed by long black hair. The first date she picked was the start of her teaching career. Then she talked about her wedding day. Next came the births of her children, two boys, three years apart. "How about one more date?" Dr. Ward said. The woman tucked a strand of hair behind her ear and began to laugh. "And in 1992," she said, "I was abgewickelt." All of the teachers burst into laughter, and so did I. Dr. Ward raised his eyebrows, his lips trying to catch this word he didn't recognize. "Abg . . . abgew. . . . Abge . . . what?" More laughter. Finally, after a minute or so, the woman explained. "Abgewickelt, you know . . . fired, let go . . . no more teaching." Dr. Ward nodded. "Ahhh," he said, and then nodded again. Another wave of laughter traveled around the room.

The laughter didn't really stop after that. During the last exercise it kept starting up in different corners. And even at the end of the lecture, as the teachers put on their coats and tucked away their notes, thanking us for coming, it was still there, following them out into the hall, erupting a couple more times as they climbed down the stairs.

Dr. Ward was pleased with how the day had gone. He counted the teachers we had seen and scribbled the number on one of the handouts. Since it was too late to return to the office, he told me to drop him off at his house in Berlin-Zehlendorf and take the station wagon home with me. I had been to his house once before. It stood close to the U.S. military base, and most of the neighbors were American diplomats or high-ranking soldiers. Dr. Ward lived with his Turkish wife, whom he had met on his last assignment in Ankara. A couple of weeks earlier, his Turkish mother-in-law had joined them. She didn't speak any English, and Dr. Ward spoke no Turkish. From what I understood, they relied on a system of hand signs. I pulled into Dr. Ward's driveway. He reached into the backseat for his coat and climbed out of the car. Before he closed the door he put his head inside again. "Good work," he said. "We'll write this up tomorrow."

I slipped the car back into traffic and followed the signs for Charlottenburg. It was dark by now, past rush hour, and the city lights were visible from the Avus highway. "Abgewickelt," I said. The word felt new, its sounds walking my mouth. I tried it again. "Abgewickelt." I knew what the word meant. It could mean to unroll something from a spool. Or to put the finishing touches on a business deal. But in the word-emptiness of reunification it had also taken on the meaning of restructuring eastern German industries, hospitals, schools, and universities, streamlining them until they fit or ceased to exist. The word was everywhere, all over the papers, but that night it felt new — filled with a teacher's defiance. A cartoon word, absurd, always off the mark.

Over the next two months, Dr. Ward and I were on the road almost every week. Some of our trips we managed in a day, but many required overnight stays. We slept in hotels whenever we could find one, which didn't happen all that often. Sometimes we stayed at university guest houses, sometimes we ended up in student dorms. Once, in Leipzig, we rented a private apartment from an old woman, a retired acrobat, who moved in with a friend during our stay. A lot of eastern Germans rented out their apartments or rooms; it was an easy way to make some extra money while things were in transition and waves of westerners kept coming through. The apartment in Leipzig was lined with black-

and-white pictures of acrobats performing their feats — a juggler, a contortionist, a woman managing a handstand on a galloping horse. Dr. Ward took over the bedroom, while I spread out my sleeping bag in the living room. On the morning of our departure, Dr. Ward pulled the shower curtain so hard that it came down, together with the metal cable that had anchored it in the wall and a fist-sized clump of plaster. I had no idea what to do. In the end, I folded up the curtain, and left it, with cable, plaster, and a note of apology, on the breakfast table.

Most of the time we traveled by car. The trains were reliable, but the connections could get complicated in some of the smaller towns. We also usually had too many things to carry. The box of USIA publications alone weighed as much as a full suitcase. And if we had scheduled several meetings in a row, which we tried to do whenever possible, there would be four or five other boxes filled with handouts and exercises. Dr. Ward liked to drive, especially on the long stretches of highway. Since he wasn't very tall, he had to scoot the seat all the way forward to reach the gas pedal, which he pressed and released at regular intervals and for no apparent reason. It sent the car into a choppy rocking motion that I at first mistook for engine trouble. My responsibility on the road was to read the maps. I liked being the navigator because it gave me more time to fill out the grid that was still unfinished in my head. With my fingers inching along highways, I could arrange cities and villages and rivers inside the new shape of my country.

As the weeks went by, Dr. Ward's presentation about our office became more polished, a set performance that he nevertheless managed to give with enthusiasm. I too knew my cues by heart. The sequence of handouts was no longer something I had to think about, and that left me more time trying to read faces. I was eager to know how we fared behind the teachers' eyes. No matter where we showed up, we were received with courtesy, and we often found ourselves invited for coffee and cake after the presentation. But there was a dividing line, a perceptible rift, between those teachers who sought us out and those who stayed aloof, watching us like curiosities. Dr. Ward and I weren't sure what to make of this. Our goal was to find the teachers who would most likely stay on, who would survive the transition and could become long-term contacts. Only we had little to go on in this search. The evaluation committees hadn't finished their work, and the new states were still busy defining their education policies, deciding how many teachers they could afford to hire or retrain. It was a mess, and it made everyone nervous. All we could do was rely on our first and second impressions — a shoddy method at best.

The teachers who ignored us might be the ones to hang on, men and women of integrity who thought it best to check us out before committing to anything new. And the ones who showed such interest, treating us to coffee and making plans for the future, could be out of work in a month. Some of them might even be playing us. A connection to the United States Information Agency might be helpful in convincing others that one had always been critical of the Socialist regime; it could suggest open-mindedness that might turn out to be useful in front of an evaluation committee. I had no proof of this, but it seemed possible. Just as we didn't know much about the teachers, they didn't know much about us. It was conceivable they mistook Dr. Ward for someone with real influence, someone connected to the people now making the decisions. I didn't like the idea of relying on blind guesses, no matter on what side. I resented my own part in this game, but found it impossible to stop trying out stories on the men and women we met, wondering whether any of them had actually worked for the State Security Police, whether such a past could show in a look or handshake.

What increased the strangeness of these encounters was that all of them took place in English. Occasionally, I would exchange a few German words with one of the teachers before or after our meeting, but those were brief interludes, never long enough to turn into a conversation. I had always enjoyed speaking English, enjoyed its ability to contain me in a different place where I too felt different and things took shape from new angles. But now I grew impatient with it. As we traveled north into Brandenburg and Mecklenburg-Vorpommern, and then south into Thuringia, Saxony-Anhalt, and Saxony, English felt more and more like a badly made coat, coarse and tight, with too little room to move.

I felt this especially one afternoon in Erfurt, where Dr. Ward gave a lecture in front of nearly two hundred former Russian teachers. Every language teacher had been forced to study Russian, but these teachers had made it their main subject and now faced the daunting task of switching to English years and even decades into their careers. Many of them spoke just a few words of English, and it was clear that hardly any of them stood a chance of mastering their new subject well enough to return to the classroom. Dr. Ward knew this too, but he didn't allow it to show that afternoon. Once again he pulled out exercise after exercise and sent his listeners into group work by yelling "action" like a madcap director. I scurried up and down the auditorium, keeping everyone supplied with handouts. A couple of times I repeated Dr. Ward's instructions to some of the teachers who didn't understand all of the words. And in those moments, speaking English, I felt embarrassed. There was no point to this lecture, to having these men and women sit through two hours of exercises they wouldn't use. Speaking English, I felt like a salesman trying to push his wares, knowing they were of little value. I wanted to stop and slow down into German, into words that seemed to promise a chance of shortening the distance between us.

One of the last places we visited, about a week after our trip to Erfurt, was the University of Halle in Saxony-Anhalt. It was one of the few trips we took by train. Outside the station we flagged down a taxi, and the driver helped us get our boxes stowed away. "Where to?" he asked as we climbed into the car. I had the university's address memorized, but I didn't give it to the driver. From my phone conversation with the department chair I knew that the English faculty had shared a building with the State Security Police, an odd coincidence that had led to an absurd nickname for the place. It had become known as the "Stasianeum," a word that combined "Stasi," the shorthand for State Security Police, and a Latin ending that made it sound like an institution of higher learning. I had chuckled with the department chair when she told me; I wanted her to know that I understood and was aware of the delicate irony involved. And now, as the driver asked where we needed to go, it was that word that came back to me. Maybe it came back because the driver seemed friendly, ready for a chat, and I thought this word could move things along, show him that I was more than a tourist. Maybe it came back because it looked like a chance to cut through the layers of English I felt wrapped around me. "Where to?" the driver asked, and I answered: "To the Stasianeum, please."

We didn't pull away from the curb. The driver turned his head and looked at me. "Where do you want to go?" I hadn't expected to have to say anything more. "The Stasianeum," I repeated, and stumbled into a kind of explanation, my face coming apart in uncertainty. When I had finished, the driver shook his head. "I don't think that's very funny," he said. He checked the side mirror, set the indicator, and pulled out into the traffic. Dr. Ward shot a quick glance at me, raising his eyebrows as if to inquire about what just happened. I pretended not to notice and leaned back into my seat, my face burning. We drove the rest of the way in silence.

Our meeting with the faculty went well. Afterward, the chair suggested getting together for dinner with some of her colleagues, and we gladly accepted. Our train back to Berlin wouldn't leave until the next day, and Dr. Ward and I had spent enough dinners by ourselves. We met at seven o'clock. The chair brought along three other teachers and also the department secretary, which was a pleasant surprise. The professors at the University of Hamburg, where I had been an undergraduate, would not have crossed that line, mingling with staff outside of work. But here it didn't look like an unusual gesture; the secretary was one of the group, joking and bantering with the others, clearly at ease. I ended up sitting next to her. For a while, Dr. Ward kept everyone entertained with stories about his time in Turkey, and then the teachers began to talk about trips they had taken after the Wall came down. One of them had been to Austria on a hiking tour. Another had made it to Venice, and she described a late night gondola trip when the city had seemed like a mirage to her, a collection of shadows. The secretary tried to follow the conversation with what little English she had. When she started looking lost, I leaned over and translated.

Soon we dropped out of the rest of the conversation, and she told me about one of her own trips — a short visit to Hamburg. I laughed and told her that Hamburg was my hometown, that my whole family still lived there.

"How did you like it?" I asked. She thought about this for a moment.

"Oh, it was fine," she said. "It's a big place, isn't it?"

"Yes, pretty big."

I was pleased to talk about Hamburg, because I missed it. Berlin was still too strange for me. I liked the capital, but its pace left me breathless, a wave always breaking right above my head.

"So what did you do in Hamburg?"

"Well, we really only had one day," she said. "We were downtown."

"Yes?"

"It was nice, but. . . ." She took a sip of wine. I did too.

"I'm sure it felt different from Halle," I said.

"It scared me."

"What did?"

"Hamburg."

For a second, an image of Hamburg lit up in my mind. There was the downtown lake, a sheet of blue filled with sailboats. Behind it, the silhouette of the Rathaus, its clock tower reaching into the sky. Not far from the Rathaus, at the corner of Jungfernstieg and Mönckebergstraße, a wooden table under a brick arch, rows of white paper bags, the smell of roasted almonds.

"What scared you?"

"Oh, I'm not sure . . . I . . . It was very big, but . . . just the way it felt, I guess." She shrugged her shoulders and smiled as if to apologize.

I nodded. "Well, it is a big place."

"Yes," she said, "it is a big place."

We both found something to look at on our plates. Then Dr. Ward started another story about his time in Turkey, and we leaned forward to listen.

Back at the office, we kept busy writing up reports about each of our trips. Dr. Ward provided the text, and I put it into the right format to adhere to the rules for official cable traffic. It was an elaborate procedure, which required strict attention to the size of margins and the spacing between paragraphs. Most of our cables went to USIA headquarters in Washington, D.C., with copies going to embassies throughout eastern Europe. Dr. Ward liked to send cables to as many posts as possible, putting into action his belief that only a reported trip was a trip that had taken place.

To ensure our visibility within the USIA hierarchy, our reports began to fill with the hard empirical evidence of our labor — "RETO Ward and FSN Lueth just completed a 650-kilometer, five-day, four-city tour of Erfurt, Jena, Gera, and Chemnitz during first week of February." "RETO spoke to over three hundred teachers during five presentations and workshops." Dr. Ward also had a knack for coming up with enticing subject headings. He wrote about "explosive demands," "tremendous challenges," and when we received news about a high-level staff change at Potsdam University, he called it a "stunning upheaval." Occasionally, he found a way to remember his rival, Dr. Frankl, reporting that the British Council had a low profile with USIA target audiences. And once, after a three-city tour through Mecklenburg-Vorpommern, I found out that I had been part not of an educational enterprise but of an "English teaching blitz."

When the first round of visits had ended and most of the cables had been written, Dr. Ward traveled to the Czech Republic and Slovakia for two weeks, taking care of the rest of his territory. I stayed at the office and wrote follow-up letters to the department chairs, thanking them again for their time and interest. It was a nice break from being on the road, and I enjoyed planning the days at my own leisure. But when Dr. Ward returned, the pace picked up again. He wanted to move ahead with recruiting U.S. English teaching fellows; he wanted to get started on the newsletter; but most of all, he wanted to put together an English teaching conference, something on a grand scale, something that would bring together teachers from all over eastern Europe, something to remember. At first, I thought the conference plan would disappear again, another blip on Dr. Ward's radar that was constantly crowded with projects. This time I was wrong. Over the next five months the conference became the center of our activities, keeping Dr. Ward awake at night as he wrote out long lists of things to do, lists that he would wave at me like a flag when he arrived at the office.

He managed to secure a USIA grant for the conference, and after considering different sites, we decided in favor of Potsdam University. The campus was close to Berlin, and it was beautiful. Several of its structures dated back to the eighteenth century, built by a defiant Frederick the Great after the Seven Years' War. None of the buildings were in perfect repair, but that only heightened their picturesque appeal. Dr. Ward declared it the right kind of backdrop for a groundbreaking event. It wasn't hard to get the faculty involved. Our main contact, Dr. Klemm, was excited about the project, and she promised to approach the university president and the state ministry for additional funds. Meanwhile, Dr. Ward wrote more cables, sending regular conference updates to Washington, keeping his superiors informed. He also spent a lot of time on the phone, calling posts in Warsaw, Prague, and Bratislava. The German phone system had improved over the past few months, but any call going eastward out of the country was still unpredictable. Through the open office door I could hear Dr. Ward hit the phone buttons in growing anger, sometimes muttering curses under his breath. When one of the calls went through, his voice would fill with relief — "Mike . . . is that you, Mike? Thank God!" — and he sounded like a man who had found his brother in a crowd of strangers.

Soon we took regular trips to Potsdam University. Most of our meetings took place in Dr. Klemm's office, where six or seven of us, clipboards and pens in hand, would crowd around a small coffee table. The closer we got to the event, the more tense the meetings became. Dr. Ward grew nervous and impatient. He knew that his Berlin assignment would be judged a success or failure depending, in large part, on the outcome of the conference. And by now our cables had spread the news and raised expectations. Some two hundred teachers from nine countries would descend on Potsdam, and it was Dr. Ward's task to keep it all together. His worries made him suspicious of Dr. Klemm and her colleagues, their ability to stay ahead of schedule and pull through. Up to this point, he had treated them with respect, but now his behavior became domineering. His list of things to do grew even longer, and he didn't hesitate to share his sense of urgency. Had someone thought about setting up coffee machines for the breaks? Who had been assigned to mark the restrooms so they would be easy to find? One by one, the teachers disappeared into Dr. Ward's anxiety. He no longer saw them as adults but as children whose self-reliance had been flattened by forty years of socialism, leaving them helpless like newly hatched birds. After one meeting, frustrated with the lack of progress, Dr. Ward threw up his arms in the parking lot and then dropped them in resignation. "These people," he said, "these people don't know shit from shinola."

But they did. Step by step, the conference started coming together. Dr. Klemm located additional funds, and she refused to get caught up in Dr. Ward's worries. In fact, she pushed back, reassuring him with platitudes as if he was the one out of the loop. She seemed to welcome this chance to prove that she and her colleagues knew what they were doing, that all that talk about easterners being unprepared for the realities of reunification was wrong, a failure to look hard enough at their lives. During our meetings, she had a difficult time hiding her displeasure when Dr. Ward went on another roll. She never interrupted him, but I could see the tension moving through her body. She sat at the edge of her seat, her back and shoulders perfectly straight, her face trying for calmness but missing it somewhere around her lips. Occasionally, she shot glances at the other teachers, which they returned with what looked to me like agreement, a pact to stay quiet for now, to wait until this was over and they could talk, maybe even have a good laugh.

I found it excruciating to watch this quiet exchange, and I wanted to be part of it. I wanted proof that they saw a difference between me and Dr. Ward. I wanted to be recognized, if not as a countryman then at least as a man who made an effort to understand what he saw and heard, who had no use for condescension. I squirmed in my seat, hoping to draw a glance, and when Dr. Klemm finally did include me, I didn't hold back. I rolled my eyes, shrugged my shoulders, and inhaled with a measured hint of exasperation.

The conference was a success. For three days, the campus came alive with teachers rushing to presentations, discussing ideas in hallways, on stairs, in the cafeteria, on the buses taking them to and from their hotels. Most of it happened in English, but there were sparks of other languages — German, Czech, Slovak, Hungarian, Polish, and also Russian. All of the publishers had fulfilled their promises, and the textbook exhibit outside the main lecture hall was well-stocked. The international panel discussion by telephone went off without problems, the voices from Arizona and Vermont coming in clear and crisp. A few things, of course, did go wrong. Three of the keynote speakers missed the bus to the opening reception. One of the hotels mixed up the room assignments. And two teachers from Hungary cornered me on the first day, complaining that I had forgotten their academic titles in the conference program. I smiled at them, apologized, and told them there was nothing I could do about it now.

By the time the last talk ended on Sunday, I could feel my concentration slip and make room for tiredness. The final week before the conference had been frantic, and now I was ready to let down my guard, to coast through what was left of a job gone right. The buses for taking the participants to the train stations started arriving, and I watched the teachers hand their luggage to the drivers, say good-bye to each other, pull out pieces of paper to write down another address. Christian Uhl, one of Dr. Klemm's colleagues, came out of the main building and joined me. "Looks like we've done it," he said in German, and his face must have resembled mine, content and mellow. He had been one of the most active faculty members working on the conference, always ready to help out. I liked him. He had a quick wit and never hesitated to ask questions. His glasses seemed to underline his inquisitiveness, a pair of wire-rims that made his eyes look slightly bigger, as if they hated to miss anything.

Herr Uhl was able to speak fluent British English, just like Dr. Klemm. I had asked him about his accent a few days before the conference, when we had spent an afternoon together preparing campus maps. It had been a simple job that left us plenty of time to chat, and since Dr. Ward wasn't around we did so in German. That afternoon Herr Uhl told me about listening to BFBS, the British Forces broadcasting from West Berlin. But he had also found other ways to sharpen his skills. Once, when the university had hosted a British family, he had volunteered to watch their two children throughout the day. It was his private language camp, he said. He talked to the children as much as he could, knowing they wouldn't flatter him. When he used the wrong words or made them sound funny, the children didn't pretend to understand. They scrunched up their faces, and he knew what still needed work. For a while, he had also helped out as an advisor to a Potsdam film studio that made English teaching videos. His responsibility was to make Potsdam look like London, and he spent hours studying movies and pictures to get the props just right. It was an easy job to get lost in, he said, to dream about at night. When he took his first trip to England a month after the Wall came down, he still couldn't shake that job. He had looked at the countryside from his train window, and for a moment he saw another movie set, quite real and convincing.

The teachers continued to hand their luggage to the drivers, huddling in small groups, saying good-bye. Maja, a German coworker from the Amerika Haus, was making her way from group to group. She was carrying a small bag, a stray piece of luggage someone must have left in the lecture hall. She had started working in the Amerika Haus a few weeks earlier and had agreed to help during the conference.

"You know, it's funny," Herr Uhl said. "For a few days I thought you and Maja were brother and sister."

"You're kidding," I said. "Why?" As far as I could tell, we didn't look very much alike. Maja was about my age, but that hardly seemed enough of a reason.

"Well, it's the way you move, I think. And, of course, the way you talk."

"The way we move? Talk?" I looked at him.

"Yes," he said, "but don't get me wrong. It's just something I've noticed about young westerners, like you two. A kind of directness in your words, a kind of confidence that just seems to be there."

I didn't know what to say. And before I could think of anything, one of the Polish teachers stood in front of us, shaking Herr Uhl's hand. I looked back at Maja, who was still moving from group to group, searching for the owner of the bag. I felt startled, my arms and legs afloat—the lines of my body no longer inevitable. And the same was true of the words in my head. They hung suspended, out of order, the distance between them and the things they named no longer certain. A lot of the words I didn't recognize, and I knew that, no matter what else, I would do well to study them with care.

Labyrinth

As I leave the Metro station, I have to check my map to make sure I know where I'm going. My destination is Normannenstraße, a small side street in Berlin-Lichtenberg and one of Germany's most infamous addresses. Until reunification, Normannenstraße was home to the headquarters of the East German Ministry for State Security, or Stasi, the gargantuan apparatus whose 260,000 full- and part-time members covered the country from one end to the other, tracking the private lives of more than six million men and women. Almost daily the papers print new revelations about the Stasi, its octopuslike reach into all layers of East German society. The beloved bishop, code name "Ingo," who spied on his own church for thirty years. The bullying of homosexuals. The recruitment of children. The high number of informers among poets and writers, whose love for words proved no moral compass at all. It is hard not to feel dizzy surrounded by such stories. My friends and I talk about what we read in the papers, and even though we know these are historical facts, we can't quite shake the feeling of following a third-rate movie script. Everything is a touch too fantastic.

I find Normannenstraße without a problem. What I don't find is the entrance to the former Stasi headquarters, which, according to my Berlin tourist guide, has been turned into a research and memorial center. I circle the entire block, looking for a sign that might point me in the right direction, but all I see are the gray facades of six- and seven-story buildings interrupted by an occasional gate. Finally, I enter one of the gates and am surprised to find more buildings, a maze of right angles and small compounds. I ask a woman rushing past me, but she just shakes her head, mumbles, "Don't know, sorry," and disappears around a corner. I have better luck with the next person, a man in his fifties, carrying a small briefcase. "The memorial center?" he repeats my question. "Well, you are close." All I have to do, he explains, is to keep walking in the same direction and then take a left after I have passed two more buildings. I follow his instructions, and they turn out to be right.

The building looks like all the others — seven stories, a perfect symmetry of gray cement and windows. The only difference I can see is that it looks even more run-down, untouched by any signs of renovation. I'm not disappointed, but I have to stretch my imagination to believe this was the place from which Erich Mielke, Minister for State Security, directed his meticulous empire. I enter through a double-set of glass doors and find myself standing in front of a scale model of the area I was just lost in. Each model building has been painted cement gray and each has been labeled with a number on its roof. There are forty-eight buildings total, spread out over two city blocks. There is also a soccer field with a running track. I locate the Metro station, retrace my roundabout walk, and realize that I have been inside the Stasi headquarters ever since I got off the train.

There is a five-Mark charge to get into the memorial center. While the man behind the cash register counts out my change, a group of twenty or so visitors has gathered behind me, ready to follow their guide up to the exhibit on the second floor. I decide to join them, and together we begin to shuffle up the black marble stairs. Photographs line the walls. Most of them were taken in the first weeks of 1990, when several thousand Berliners forced their way into the Stasi complex at night, trying to prevent the destruction of secret files. The pictures show broken windows and documents scattered across floors like snow. In the glare of flashlights, people's faces glow with stonelike determination. A little farther up the stairs, another set of pictures shows only graffiti, slogans smeared against the walls of the headquarters. Most of the slogans I have seen before on other buildings throughout the city — "Stasi Get Out" or "We are the people." But one graffiti surprises me because it is specific instead of abstract: "You have killed Matthias Domaschk." I don't recognize the name, but now I can't stop wondering how he died, whether he was shot during an attempted escape, or maybe sentenced to death at a mock trial.

"Please move up. That way I don't have to shout." Our guide ushers us into a long, narrow hallway. She is a woman in her midthirties, dressed in a white cotton dress and tennis shoes. Her long, brown hair is kept in place by a white headband. "We have now reached the floor on which Erich Mielke and his secretarial staff resided." Our group listens quietly as she starts listing figures and outlines the work that was done here. Several times she begins her explanations with "as we all know," and from the way she says the words with a mix of sarcasm and easy familiarity, I conclude that the group I have joined must be eastern German. I look around to double-check. Six years after reunification, clothing isn't much of a clue anymore, and I'm not sure it ever was. But a lot of us have become slipshod anthropologists these days, and even though I'm slightly embarrassed by my own action, I begin to scan the men and women standing next to me. I glance at their blouses and sweaters, checking for clashing colors and old-fashioned cuts. And I glance at their faces and postures, not knowing exactly what I'm looking for, something tentative, I think, something turned inward instead of out.

Our guide continues her short lecture. We try to keep up with the details. Some thirty-six thousand people worked in the Berlin headquarters. More than three thousand were involved in tapping phones. Every Stasi employee had a military rank, right down to the women who cleaned these rooms. We laugh when we hear the part about the cleaning women, and I imagine a stern-faced matron dusting bookshelves in uniform. When we are quiet once more, our guide tells us about the three full-time Stasi workers whose job was to shop in West Berlin, day in and day out, bringing back enemy amenities for their superiors. This sets us off again, and it takes a while until the last chuckle has died down. "You must remember that there was plenty of western currency to go around for those in power," our guide throws in. "Take Honecker, for example. Do you know what they found among the belongings of our former party chief?" She pauses for a moment to let the question sink in. "Videos, pornographic videos worth 1.3 million Marks." This time there is hardly any laughter at all, just a low murmur and some shuffling of feet.

We move into the first room off the hallway, and I take out my notepad to jot down what I've just heard. I find a place in the corner, a few feet away from the rest of the group, and rush my pen across the page. When I look up again, a man and a woman standing at the edge of the group are watching me. Our eyes meet only for a second or two before we make an effort to look somewhere else. I'm startled by their scrutiny, and although I know that I have done nothing wrong, I suddenly feel like a trespasser, like someone who has crossed the line of good taste in a place where observation was never innocent. I slide the notepad back into my shirt pocket and rejoin the group. I wonder what the man and woman are thinking about. Did they notice my running shoes? My backpack? I cross my arms in front of me, then uncross them again. I try to concentrate on our guide. I don't want anyone to doubt my good intentions.

The room we are in is a simple square, one side of it a row of large windows. Some of the windows are cracked open, allowing a slight breeze to play with the thin, white curtains. Except for three display cases, the room is empty, and it is hard to tell what its purpose used to be. Our guide calls our attention to the middle case, which contains stories of former Stasi prisoners. Each story has been typed up and slipped under a large plastic cover, and as we file past the display, we lift the covers, slowly and deliberately, like the pages of an old, oversize atlas. The story I get to read is about a woman, four years older than I. In 1986, on the twenty-fifth anniversary of the Wall, she writes a letter of complaint to Erich Honecker. She is unhappy with the political restrictions and complains about the state's shortsighted economic strategies. Five weeks after the letter, she is sentenced to sixteen months in prison under article 220 — the public insult of East German state institutions. Her story doesn't end there, but I decide to skip the last paragraph. I'm too worried about holding up the line behind me.

The next room is much smaller. It is an office with a desk and three chairs. An old TV set occupies the corner by the window, and right above it hangs a calendar frozen in time, telling us that this is December 1989. To the left of the desk stands a wardrobe, and the radio on top of it looks even older than the TV. Two bulky telephones sit next to each other on the desk, their dials smudged from frequent use. There is a grease spot on the white wallpaper behind one of the chairs. Whoever worked here must have had a habit of leaning his head against the wall when he needed to relax. "Take a look at the radio," our guide tells us. "Can you see the three white stickers on the dial?" I didn't notice the stickers before, but now they stand out, three unevenly spaced dots with handwritten letters on them. "As we all know, the airwaves above East Berlin were full of enemy signals," our guide says with a smile. "And just to make sure that nobody tuned in those signals by accident, some eager Stasi employee marked the official East German stations on this radio." We laugh. Several people in the group shake their heads, some whisper to a neighbor, and I wonder what memories they may be calling up right now. Did they have special routines when they listened to western radio or watched western television? Did they use sofa pillows to muffle the sound? Did they close curtains, or even shutters? I look back at the radio, at the dark stretches of dial between the stickers, and I'm surprised by what I already know, that the words excluded here so carefully, the words retrieved in secret by the people around me, were the same I listened to without a second thought, without ever considering them anything but ordinary.

We follow our guide through the next few rooms, most of them more offices for support staff. All of the furniture I see is simple and belongs to a different era, a mix of the late sixties and early seventies. The few pieces of office equipment also look ancient — electronic typewriters whose metal bodies swallow entire desks, switchboards with square push buttons the size of dice. In many ways, these rooms are not what I had expected. I miss a certain degree of flamboyance, a more arrogant display of power by a state ministry that claimed to know and defend the truth at all times. The dark wood of the desks and cabinets, the ornamented carpets, the lace curtains, the potted plants, all of it conjures up the atmosphere of an old-fashioned living room, the kind of place where I might listen to my great-aunt losing herself in stories about a long-gone summer. To my surprise, the familiarity of the rooms bothers me. It makes it difficult to brush the rooms off as a separate realm of evil and cling to the conviction that I would have never belonged to such a place. Studying one of the large, old-fashioned typewriters, I wonder whether I could have been one of the writers burrowing into the lives of others.

"We are now in Erich Mielke's very own office, and as you can tell it is a bit more generous than what we have seen so far." I look around the room we have just entered as our guide waits for the rest of the group to catch up. The room is about three times as large as the other ones, and the furniture has clearly been selected with more care. There is a big conference table with ten chairs and next to it a more relaxed assembly of five armchairs. All of the chairs have royal blue upholstery, which seems to glow against the deep red carpet. Mielke's desk stands near the back of the room, behind it a large safe whose door has been thrown wide open. Three heavy dial phones, one white and two black, sit on the left side of the desk. I decide that the colors must have been significant, reserved for different levels of secrecy. Opposite the phones, on the right side of the desk, is a glass cover, and at first I can't make out what it contains. I walk up closer and see that it is a death mask of Lenin, propped up at a slight angle to better display its features.

We crowd around the desk as our guide outlines the stages of Mielke's career, his thirty-two-year stint as the top Stasi officer. She then turns around, points to the open safe, and tells the story of the two briefcases Mielke kept hidden here. I have heard parts of this story before, another anecdote that could have been fiction. One of the briefcases contained documents about Erich Honecker, which proved that the party chief had been less heroic than he claimed when he was arrested by the Nazis in 1935. Instead of sticking up for his Communist beliefs, as he wrote in his official autobiography, Honecker cooperated with the Gestapo and compromised several of his comrades. "These documents were Mielke's insurance," our guide says, "something to fall back on in case his superior ever turned on him." The second briefcase concerned Mielke himself. It was full of court files about the murder of two Berlin police officers in 1931, files pointing to Mielke as one of the killers. I know about these files because they ended up as evidence in Mielke's trial after reunification, a legal drama that spilled into the papers and onto television. I remember the pictures of Mielke in the courtroom, an old man in his eighties, dressed in a dark suit, turning his head in slow motion above a stiff, white collar. He looked fragile, confused, even capable of good. In the end, he was sentenced to six years in prison for the 1931 killings. All other charges had to be dropped because of the defendant's poor health.

"Do you have any questions?" our guide asks. There is a short moment of silence. "Would you mind if I sat at his desk?" The man who asks the question is standing right next to the guide, smiling. He looks to be around forty. He is wearing a blue shirt, gray slacks, and a pair of sandals. One of his hands is already resting on the back of Mielke's chair. "Oh, sure," our guide says, "go right ahead. I don't think he would mind." The man pulls back the chair and slowly low-ers himself into it. He moves back and forth a couple of times, wriggles his shoulders into the royal blue upholstery, savoring, it seems, this belated chance to trespass. When he stops moving, he puts his hands on the desk and pretends to look around the room with an air of exaggerated dignity. "Hey, this is pretty comfortable," he finally says with a short laugh, and since we don't know what else to do, we all laugh with him.

The space right behind Mielke's office is an actual living room, once reserved for the minister's private needs. Our guide tells us that Mielke, after his release from prison last year, now lives ten minutes away in a high-rise in Berlin-Hohenschönhausen, and somehow that piece of information makes a difference in how the room feels, filling it with a tangible presence. A red-and-black plaid blanket lies neatly folded on a daybed by the window, as if someone still came here to take naps. Behind me, on the wall across from the daybed, hangs a large oil painting, the first I have seen in any of the rooms. The painting shows a forest clearing that opens onto a vista of rolling hills. Near the horizon, the hills change from green to blue, framing the narrow band of a lake. In the foreground, massive oak trees lean into the clearing like pillars and cast a ring of shadow. A single hunter and his dog stand just outside the trees, and when I look for the first time, they seem to have no purpose, standing still as if to take in the view. Only when I look again, a minute later, do I see the deer on the opposite side of the clearing, a faint streak suspended in the shadows, straining for cover.

Part of Mielke's private quarters is a bathroom, and it doesn't take long until someone asks the guide for permission to go in. Soon a small line forms in front of the door. I'm not sure what to make of this. Why would anyone want to see Mielke's bathroom? I don't understand this sudden interest, but I take my place in line nevertheless. As much as I would like to believe that my reason for visiting the memorial center is only benign, a healthy desire to understand the past, I also recognize another element in it. The Stasi story with all of its absurd twists has triggered a voyeur's curiosity in me; I am like a moviegoer ready to be thrilled from the safety of his seat. I might miss something inside that bathroom. Maybe one of the bulky telephones has been installed next to the toilet. Maybe the mirror above the sink is fake and once allowed the secret supervision of Mielke's own staff.

The line edges forward, and my first glimpse is of the toilet, set off by itself in a small room. I look around but find nothing out of the ordinary. The pipe behind the toilet must have been leaking for a long time, leaving a wrinkled, rust-colored vein on the blue tiles. Up ahead I can see the rest of the bathroom, a larger space containing a tub, a sink, and a separate shower. Two men and a woman stand huddled together next to the sink, and from the way they are pointing at the walls and nodding occasionally, I can tell that something has caught their attention. I move up closer, trying to make out their words. "I don't remember ever seeing this kind before," says one of the men, letting his hand slide across a section of the wall above the tub. "You don't?" says the other, "seems to me that those first came out in the seventies." I look back at the wall, at the very spot the man's hand has just touched, but I can't see anything. "The worst part was never knowing what color you'd get," says the woman. "If you wanted green, you'd get white. That is, if you got anything at all." "Yes," the first man agrees, "we never once got the colors we wanted," and by then I have realized they are talking about tiles. And almost at the same time I recall what I have heard about tiles in East Germany, that they were hard to come by, a prized possession in a black market where tiles might be exchanged for car parts, which could be traded for house paint, which in turn might be swapped for window frames. Neither the two men nor the woman are thinking about Mielke and his Stasi right now. They are not even in the same room with me; they are trading memories, details of an earlier life that is gone and of which I still understand very little. As I slip out of the bathroom, I can hear the traces of nostalgia in their voices.

It is on the next floor, which we reach via another flight of black marble stairs, that the memorial center catches up with my imagination. Here, in the first of two rooms, the everyday tools of secret surveillance line up along the walls. A collection of fountain pens lies neatly arranged under glass, each one a microphone with a thin electric cord growing out of one end. An old metal watering can lies tipped on its side, a hole in its bottom revealing the hidden camera. Another camera has been lodged inside a birdhouse, and yet another nestles inside a gas can. Next to the gas can lies a gnarled tree root, the size of a man's arm, and it too contains a camera, this one looking out through two tiny drill holes. Most of the equipment I see is simple, keeping the eye from getting distracted by the sleek exterior of high technology. No such smoke screen exists here. The simplicity of the tools, the almost baroque wires and switches, convey undiluted purpose: to do violence to another person's dignity.

Our guide points to the birdhouse and the tree root. She reminds us that East Berliners had a habit of leaving their apartments when they wanted to speak their minds without fear. They took walks through the city, they found quiet corners in parks, and the Stasi tried to keep up, hiding cameras in birdhouses and tree roots. Once again I notice heads nodding, eyes going out of focus inside of memories. This time, I find a memory of my own: a weeklong high school trip, more than fourteen years ago, which took me and fifteen other students to Radebeul, a small town outside of Dresden. We had spent a semester studying East Germany, and the trip was supposed to balance out the theory, all the charts and statistics our teacher had prepared for us. We traveled by train, and as we approached the border, most of us felt nervous, digging through our bags well ahead of time to make sure we'd have our papers ready. After the checkpoint, proud of the brand-new stamp in our West German passports, we sat glued to the train windows. We stared at the villages and the people waiting at train crossings. We called each other's attention to whatever looked different, the missing paint on houses, the long stretches of cobblestone streets, the odd shape of street lamps. And, of course, we laughed at the two-cycle Trabants, toy cars sputtering and shaking their way through the countryside in clouds of blue smoke.

It wasn't until we had left the train in Dresden that we noticed the middle-aged man with glasses and a briefcase who followed us through the station and didn't make much of an effort to hide his intention. Wherever we went, he went also, standing about twenty yards away, watching us in short, birdlike intervals. Someone in our group remembered seeing the man already on the train, which in all likelihood meant he had been trailing us since the border. At first, we only stole a few glances at him. But as the wait for our connecting train grew longer, we gradually became bolder with our own gazes, meeting his head-on. We joked about the contents of his briefcase. A walkie-talkie. A secret file with our names. Maybe a gun. But in spite of the jokes and the secret agent poses we struck in front of each other, we weren't fully at ease. The man's insistence, his refusal to let our stares bother him, took us by surprise, and it brought home the fact that he had been following us with adult purpose. He was observing us, while all we could do was look back. It wasn't the same thing at all, and somehow we felt the difference, understood that our actions had taken on new meaning on this side of the border. We didn't put any of this into words then. We simply continued with our jokes and poses, but I also remember that we stayed close together, suddenly indifferent to our elaborate high school hierarchies, grateful for the familiarity of each other's faces.

After our return home, we invited our parents to school for an evening of presentations about our trip. We put together a small booklet of articles, most of them brief introductions to the history of Dresden and its tourist attractions: The firebombing of February 13 and 14, 1945. The Zwinger Palace with its collection of old masters. The porcelain factory in nearby Meißen. It was an odd mix, a kind of random collage, which we pasted together by stealing large chunks of stilted language from encyclopedias and dictionaries. To loosen up the design of our publication, we scattered hand-drawn political slogans throughout the texts. They were the same slogans we had seen in the streets of Dresden, printed on large banners or painted on the walls of houses: *The Teachings Of Karl Marx Are Powerful Because They Are True. Peace And Socialism Have To Be Armed. Theory Turns Into Material Force When It Captures The Masses.* My contribution was an essay about our arrival at the Dresden station. I wrote about the Russian soldiers who had filed past us on the platform. I called them "short and stocky" and wondered about their Asian features. I wrote about the four or five policemen who had broken up a group of chanting soccer fans with the help of dogs and then dragged one of the men away for questioning. And I wrote about the middle-aged man with glasses who had stuck to us like a shadow, drilling his eyes into our facade of self-confidence. My goal was to create an uneasy, even oppressive atmosphere, and then, at the end of the essay, I contrasted it all with one of the political slogans I had seen at the station: *The Stronger Our Socialism, The Stronger Our Peace.* I liked the irony behind the juxtaposition, and my friends agreed that it was a clever ending.

I don't know whether our parents read what we handed out to them that night. I think it likely they just leafed through it, more proud than interested, pleased with the hard evidence of our learning. For many of us the trip had been our first visit to East Germany, and it had given us the chance to see the country as a place of three dimensions. But I don't remember this more mature vision becoming a reality for us. If we had felt connected to East Germany in the way of countrymen and women, then it had happened in momentary, unexpected niches. A street corner conversation. A familiar joke at a bus stop. The name of a dish scrawled in chalk outside a restaurant. But mostly what we saw and heard came at us filtered, flattened out by the pressures of opposing ideologies. At eighteen, we arrived in Dresden with the seamless self-confidence that comes from a lack of experience, and that attitude found its counterpart in the smug official posture of our tour guide — a woman in her early thirties, who, among other things, told us that East Germany had no problem with alcoholism, that, in fact, there wasn't a single alcoholic in a population of sixteen million. Socialism, she said, made such secondhand escapes unnecessary. We rolled our eyes at her and laughed. But we also felt provoked. Our reactions alternated between shrugging her off as a lunatic and trying to argue with her, filled with a missionary zeal we didn't know we had. In the end, our trip didn't create any lasting ties, nothing that might have led us to reconsider the boundaries of our belonging. Of course, we had plenty of opinions about what we had seen. And, in theory, we all agreed with the need for reunification, but we didn't expect it to happen in our lifetime. It was as remote a possibility as we could imagine, and standing in front of our parents that night at school, dressed up and nervous, we told our stories like true travelers, who had just made it back from the unknown.

The last room of the exhibit contains a replica of a prison cell — a heavy wooden door with three locks, a peephole, and a slot for food and mail; behind the door a plank-bed with a couple of sheets in a plastic bag; behind the bed a life-size photograph of grimy, water-damaged walls and a heavily barred window near the ceiling, letting in a bit of daylight. Across the room, two display cases show pieces of prisoners' clothing, one of which is a rough denim suit marked with a yellow stripe on arm and leg. There is also a denim shirt, which has the yellow stripe running down the center of the back. "What you see here," our guide says, "is one of the cells from the Stasi prison in Berlin-Hohenschönhausen." She tells us that the more brutal forms of interrogation of the fifties and sixties gave way to more psychological methods in the seventies and eighties. "Let me give you an example," she says and describes the case of a young man whose interrogators wore him down by making him listen to the screams of a woman, telling him that the sounds came from his pregnant girlfriend in the next room. "Are there any questions?" our guide asks after a brief pause. We stand spread out in a circle along the walls. Nobody has a question. One of the windows is open, and the breeze plays with the lace curtain, pushing it into the room like a pillar of smoke.

"What very few people know," our guide continues, "is that the Stasi had plans for isolation camps all over the country in case of a political crisis. Some eighty-six thousand citizens, people the Stasi considered unreliable, would have ended up in these camps surrounded by barbed wire and watchtowers." We listen quietly. I have never heard of this before. Our guide recommends a book about the camps, and I carefully write down both author and title. I will buy the book a few days later, a slim volume with a plain cover. One of the chapters will discuss the term *liquidation* as it appears in official government documents about the camps. The chapter will conclude that the term's semantic reach remains unclear.

We have come to the end of our tour, but our circle doesn't break up right away. We are caught under the weight of what we have heard. Finally, a young man in a short-sleeved shirt steps into the center of the room and puts out his hand to the guide. "Thank you so much. That was very interesting," he says. "I just wanted to tell you that over in the West, where I'm from, some of the government offices still have the same kind of furniture you have here." Our guide nods, surprised, her lips experimenting with a smile. "How about that," she says. "Who would have thought we had that much in common." And then one of us begins to laugh, not very loud at all, but soon another person joins in, and then another, and before long the whole room is full of this laughter we don't quite understand.

Walk Don't Walk

Berlin has been condemned always to become, never to be.
— Karl Scheffler, 1910

I dial Berlin Tourist Information. My fingers dance across the phone, and when I put the receiver to my ear, I hear the faint buzz of electricity homing in on my destination. Then the signal. Then a woman's voice, friendly and caring. "All our lines are busy right now. Please do not hang up. We will take your call as soon as one of our representatives is available. Thank you." Then the music sets in, the voice of a man and a woman climbing and falling alongside violins and trumpets. I'm not surprised to find myself on hold. Berlin is a busy place these days. I remember the year I had to find an apartment in the city, not too long after the Wall had vanished. Friends told me it might take six months, if I were lucky, or maybe a year, if I weren't. I placed a want ad in *Der Tagesspiegel*, and when I told the woman that I hadn't thought of offering a finder's fee, she laughed at me, her high-pitched giggle a mix of cosmopolitan disbelief and pity. "Well, you might as well forget it then," she said, and I felt found out, a man from the provinces learning the ropes of the capital.

"All our lines are busy right now. Please do not hang up. We will take your call as soon as one of our representatives is available. Thank you." This time I just want to visit, walk around, look for the city that boasts of being the workshop of German Unity. I haven't been back for three years. The man and the woman still sing with unflagging enthusiasm. They sing about Berlin, and the tune is easy and smooth, half Sinatra, half Olympic theme song. The words are English, which surprises me at first but then makes sense. Some tourists may feel stranded in a language they don't understand. They might get bored and hang up, which wouldn't do. From a statistical point of view, English has to be the safest bet. And it is safe in another way. After all, this is Berlin, the old and new German capital, where history settles in thick layers, and too much celebration, too much pride, might seem unnerving to some. English, well-lit and democratic, provides assurance. "This is the city of friends," the man and the woman sing and then get cut off by the other recording, the one that tells me I haven't been forgotten. Piece by piece the lyrics slide into my receiver, no longer quite fitting together, a collage of happiness and goodwill—"one day they broke down the Wall" and "harmony in our hearts" and "now we are walking hand in hand." The last line I hear before my call goes through is this one:

"The dream can now begin."

The S-Bahn rattles into Friedrichstraße station. On a whim, I decide to get off and take a taxi the rest of the way. It's a warm day, and I'm tired of lugging my bag around. The driver nods when he hears the name of my hotel and pulls out into the traffic. We travel south on Friedrichstraße, then turn east onto Unter den Linden. "What the heck is that?" I say, more to myself than to the driver, but he's glad to have an opening. "You mean the pipes?" he asks, and looks at me in the rearview mirror. "Yes," I answer and stare out the window. All along Unter den Linden, at a height of fifteen feet, pink and blue metal pipes run parallel to the sidewalks. They span intersections and fork off into side streets without an end in sight. They look like something out of a Jules Verne novel, a giant pneumatic mail system that pumps news capsules from one end of the city to the other. "They are water pipes," says the driver, "controlling groundwater from the construction at Potsdamer Platz." "Oh," I say and settle back into my seat.

We continue east on Unter den Linden, cross the Schloßbrücke, and drive past the Palast der Republik, the former East German parliament building. The driver finds me again in his rearview mirror. "If you ask me," he says, "there's too much construction going on. Can't believe all this was rotten. It's money, you know." I nod, wondering what part of the city he lives in. He looks fiftyish, gray hair, glasses. He drives without hurry, steady, shifting well before the engine has to strain. "You never know what streets are open. The guys on the radio should simply announce what streets haven't been torn up. Would save a lot of time." I nod again and think of the Berlin map in my backpack. I bought it a couple of days ago, and when I unfolded it to look at the layout of the city's heart, I noticed the fine print near Potsdamer Platz: *Traffic flow may change at any time.* A mapmaker's final surrender. We circle around Alexanderplatz, switch lanes a couple of times, and then pull into the driveway of the hotel. I hand over the fare and get my bag out of the trunk. "Looks like I'm in luck with the weather," I say, leaning into the driver's window. He laughs and shakes his head. "Hey, I wouldn't mind some rain," he says, "better for business." Then he puts the car in gear and slips back into the traffic.

Berlin is situated on the great plain of the North German Flatlands. Its precise geographical location is 52°31′12″ N and 13°24′36″ E. The city covers an area of 889 square kilometers. It extends 38 km from north to south and 45 km from east to west. The city lies between 34 and 60 meters above sea level. The highest elevations are the Teufelsberg in the Grunewald and the Müggelberge near Köpenick, which are 115-meter-high mounds of wartime rubble. The climate is continental and is also influenced by Atlantic seawinds. Berlin is set in a landscape of forests and woods which also cover 24 percent of the city's surface. A further 6.7 percent of the land is used for agriculture, and there are 197 km of navigable waterways in the city.

From where I stand on the roof of the INFO BOX, I can see all of Potsdamer Platz. This used to be Europe's busiest intersection, an anthill of cars, trucks, trams, carriages, bicycles, and pedestrians. In 1924, somewhere in front of me, stood Germany's first traffic light. Cafés. Hotels. The clattering of hooves. Car horns. Newspaper boys shouting headlines. After the war — a pocket of silence. The slow shuffle of black market dealers and hungry customers. Then, the growing solidity of sector lines, a fissure running through Potsdamer Platz that, on August 13, 1961, becomes the Wall, cutting the city. Now, there is so much movement I don't know which way to look: Right in front of me a giant excavator floats in the middle of a lake. (This must be the groundwater, I think.) Every two minutes or so, the excavator's shovel plunges into the water, sinks for several seconds, then comes up again, spewing muddy fountains as it breaks the surface and goes airborne. The excavator swivels, slowly and deliberately, until the shovel hangs above a barge already half full. The shovel opens and the mud rains into the barge, rocking it into a sideways dance. When the barge leaves, the construction site looks like a harbor.

I let my eyes travel upward to study the cranes, the men in their tiny control boxes. They are too far away to be real. Like weathervanes caught in a complicated wind, the cranes turn in all directions, and yet they never touch. I begin to count. Twice I have to start over because the cranes crowd each other into invisibility, mechanical knots that tighten and fall apart above the horizon. I count to fifty-two, then let my eyes come down again. Cement trucks make their way past stacks of wood and metal, each truck painted in black and white stripes. From a distance, they look like zebras whose torsos have come unhinged. A bulldozer rounds up a small mountain of ground, sending up dark smoke each time the engine climbs into another gear. When it backs up, the warning signal cuts through the air and mixes with the other sounds: The insistent staccato of jackhammers. The high whine of electrical saws. The splashing of water. A random symphony of drumbeats rolling across metal, wood, cement, and ground.

"Excuse me." There is a slight tap on my shoulder. I turn around and look at a woman holding a camera. "Would you mind taking a picture of me and my husband over here?" I look over at the husband. He reassures me with a smile. "Sure," I say and take the camera. "Everything's automatic," the woman says, putting her arm around her husband. "Just press the button." I look through the viewfinder. The couple is smiling. A bit of wind catches the woman's blue dress, and she bends over to straighten it. Then her hand moves up to her hair, tucking away a few loose strands. The husband hasn't moved. "Okay," I say, and their smiles travel ahead in time, trying to catch up with the photograph already taken in their minds. I don't press the button right away. I'm waiting for some of the cranes to move into the picture. When they finally do, I'm ready.

Berlin will soon have a beating heart again. The German capital's new urban center is rising in Potsdamer Platz. The project's dimensions are extraordinary: eighteen thousand people will live and work here; one hundred thousand visitors, guests and customers will be expected daily.

Berlin's dead heart will start to beat again as these few years pass, re-created as a pulsating, bubbling center for the twenty-first century. A myth is being reconstructed here, a new piece of metropolis is coming into being as an experiment — an experiment without historical precedent. Something that normally takes decades or centuries to evolve is being created here in only a few years.

The fall of the Wall was a victory for mankind. However, as terrible as it may sound, at the same time Berlin lost one of its main tourist attractions.

A new concept has been born in Berlin: construction site tourism.

Auguststraße. I'm looking for number 75, but I can't find it. Most of the houses on this street haven't been renovated, and the numbers aren't easily legible. The five-story-high facades run through all shades of gray, the crumbling balconies struggle with gravity. I pass a small, makeshift art gallery and decide to ask the two men sitting in front of it. They barely look up, then point to an entrance on their left. As I enter, a young woman with a baby carriage is getting ready to leave. "Excuse me, is this number 75?" I ask. "Yes," she says, smiling. I look around for mailboxes or doorbells, something to help me find the apartment I want. Nothing. The woman is bending over the carriage, straightening the blanket. "Would you happen to know where Markus Heckhausen lives?" She looks up and thinks for a moment. "I'm afraid I don't," she says and unlocks the brakes of the carriage. "You may have heard of him," I tell her, "he's a designer. He takes East German pedestrian lights and turns them into indoor lamps." She looks at me again and shakes her head. I can tell she has begun to doubt my sense of reality. "Sorry, I really don't know," she says and pushes past me.

The entrance hall of the house doesn't have any stairs. There is only one apartment door without a name, but I don't try it. I seem to remember that Markus Heckhausen talked about living on the second floor in our phone conversation. I cut through the hall and enter the courtyard, a funnel of windows and more gray walls. A door on the opposite side leads to the stairs, and I begin to climb. The banister is made from wood, worn dark and soft by a century of hands. The walls of the stairwell are pale green. Most of the paint has cracked and bends away from the moisture underneath. In the dim light, the flakes of paint look like butterflies, resting, waiting to break into a confusion of wings. Since the house is in such poor repair, the question of ownership must still be pending. Nobody will invest until there is certainty in this matter. But afterward the change will be swift, triggering a procession of painters, carpenters, brick masons, plumbers, electricians, and whoever else knows the right craft. I have seen it happen in other eastern neighborhoods, a house surrounded by a metal corset, shedding years in a matter of weeks.

Markus Heckhausen does live on the second floor. I ring the bell and a young man with tiny, round glasses opens the door. He wears a loose-fitting white sweater. His black pants are splattered with paint. "Hello," he says, "come on in." The apartment has two rooms, and the lamps are everywhere. Five or six of them sit on the floor, their white electrical cords twisting around each other like pasta. Pictures of the lamps have been taped to a large computer, which hums evenly in a pile of newspaper clippings and press releases. A box of light bulbs and a box of sockets share the sofa under a print by Monet.

"You see," Markus Heckhausen says, "I didn't like the idea of East German pedestrian lights being replaced by western ones without reason. So I decided to preserve them." He picks up one of the lamps and puts it into my hands. I can easily tell the difference between the East German lights and the West German ones I grew up with. Both use the picture of a man to tell pedestrians whether to walk or not, but the two men seem to belong to separate clans. "I think the East German man looks more dynamic, more lifelike than the western man," Markus Heckhausen says. "He deserves to survive." I study the shape of the pedestrian-light-man in front of me. He is red (don't walk), short and stocky, spreading his arms. He also wears a hat (western man doesn't), a type of fedora, which gives him the appearance of respectable middle-age. He looks like the kind of man who has his finances in order and likes to feed pigeons in the park. His green counterpart, whom I spot on the floor, also wears a hat. Like western man, he is turned sideways, walking, but his arms seem to swing with more determination and energy. "Yes," I say, "he is less abstract."

The red lamp I hold in my hands has a serrated steel rim with the English words *Don't stop me now!* cut into it. The rim around the green lamp reads: *Keep on walking* . . . Markus Heckhausen takes the lamp from me and explains where he had to file off some sharp edges to be in line with German safety regulations. "I also had to use some superglue," he says. "Keeps the socket from spinning in the frame." He puts the lamp down and hands me a press release: *The original East German pedestrian-light-man now gives his first civilian performance — as "keep on walking" in green and as "don't stop me now" in red. Since his "colleagues" are threatened with complete replacement by standardized western men, the pedestrian-light-lamp assures that a piece of eastern culture will survive in a humorous and decorative manner. After running (or standing) in the eastern parts of the country for more than thirty years, the pedestrian-light-man deserves an honorable departure and shouldn't just disappear: And that is why he now receives an imaginary victory wreath in the shape of a serrated steel rim. . . . Whoever would like to own a pedestrian-light-man can order him for 198 Marks at: Heckhausen Design, Auguststraße 75, 10117 Berlin (Mitte), Tel/Fax (030) 28 28 78 0. . . . Markus Heckhausen studied product design at the Polytechnic Institute in Pforzheim* [here I learn that he is from the West]. *A year ago he started his own business in Berlin. And in the inspiring atmosphere of a metropolis under construction, the pedestrian-light-lamp has become his first product.*

"Did you know they're planning a completely new pedestrian-light-man?" Markus Heckhausen asks. I shake my head. "Yes, and he's going to be even more abstract than the western one." He walks over to a table by the window, where the lamp parts have grown into a small pyramid. "I have one of these guys around here somewhere." He searches the pile, pulling it apart like a lump of stubborn seaweed. "Ah, here he is," he says and holds up a black plastic cover with the shape of a man carved into it. I can see what he means. This man isn't even in one piece anymore — head, torso, arms, and legs all float next to each other as if waiting for their chance to leave. "I don't like it," Markus Heckhausen says, speaking with a designer's confidence in matters of form. While he holds up the new man, I study his face and am struck by how tired he looks, his eyes disappearing behind the small glasses, the shadow of a beard across his cheeks. So far, he has put together a hundred lamps in his apartment, some fifty have been sold — not enough to pay the bills, he says. He works a couple of other jobs and eats at the university cafeteria. His car, which he bought a couple of weeks ago, is an eastern two-cycle Trabant.

Take a riksha through Berlin: An architectural excursion in a real Chinese riksha. From the Middle Ages to Prussia, from the Cold War into the next century. You will see, among other things, Unter den Linden, Pariser Platz, Potsdamer Platz, and Checkpoint Charlie.

The INFO BOX at Potsdamer Platz cost ten million Marks. On a good day it informs up to ten thousand visitors. This is my third trip to the box. Here all the investors explain what they are up to, what buildings they will move into, what architects they have hired to push their dreams into three dimensions. The box looks funny. It is bright red and sits on steel stilts eight meters above the ground. The stilts disappear into the box at different angles, which, from a distance, makes the structure look like a staggering beetle. To get into the box one has to get under the box, where a broad flight of steel stairs leads up to the first floor. Climbing the stairs, even for the third time, I have the feeling of boarding a ship, and I look at the people around me to decide whether they would make good traveling companions. Later, after reading the INFO BOX catalog, I will find out that I'm not the first one to think this. I will also receive help with my metaphor. *The INFO BOX is like a large spaceship in the middle of all the building activity. And as is only right and proper for a spaceship of this kind it has a crew. Despite all the technology, people are still needed to welcome visitors and make sure they enjoy themselves.*

Some of the crew members are on duty behind the information desk on the first floor. Two or three others are busy leading small groups through the exhibit. But mostly the visitors explore on their own. We push each other past flowcharts, cluster around display cases, touch computer screens, and click mouses. There is plenty of noise inside the box. The clatter of voices mixes with recordings that switch back and forth between music and sonorous explanations of building phases and technological challenges. Underneath the voices is the murmur of feet, thousands of them, shuffling, tapping, scraping from one floor to another. On my last two visits I learned that Potsdamer Platz is the largest inner-city building site in Europe. I also learned that it is a city in itself. It has its own road and rail system. It has its own groundwater lake. It has its own houses — tiny, yellow boxes stacked like bricks, where men fall into what must be deep, motionless slumber.

Today I spend most of my time in front of a large screen. It explains the plans for putting the city's rail system back together, for making it meet the demands of the next millennium. *Berlin's new, strong heart will be beating in the Central Area in a few years. Transport systems that will do justice to the demands of a major modern city that is additionally becoming the East-West hub at the center of Europe are being built at the same time as the innovative eco-*

nomic center of the German capital is growing up. Right now, the screen shows a computer simulation of Lehrter Bahnhof, a large station that should be finished some time after the year 2000. We hover about two hundred meters above the station, admiring its massive glass roof. A man's voice tells us that some 110,000 passenger changes will take place in Lehrter Bahnhof each day. Then our perspective begins to shift. Slowly, we tip forward and begin to gather speed. We are falling toward the glass roof. For a second or two I worry, still trapped inside of real space and gravity. But when we hit the roof it is already gone, and we now fly underneath it, sweeping above the heads of future travelers and high-speed trains waiting to leave.

Come to Berlin! The capital will never again be what it is today. Feel how the city, how its center changes daily. Take a look today at the city of tomorrow. [I do. This is what I notice: In the Berlin of the future, rising inside the memory of hard drives, the sun is always shining.]

Each time a train passes overhead, a deep rumble travels through the brick walls, and I stop eating my soup. Even after three hours of sitting in this restaurant, I'm not used to this string of ten-second earthquakes that rattle the lamp above my head and make my coffee cup dance on its saucer. I worry that the walls are going to give. They were built in 1882, part of a five-mile viaduct running through Berlin's center from east to west, and look, as far as I can tell, in need of repair. It wasn't my idea to come here. Cornelia suggested the place, which she remembers from her student days in East Berlin. She is drinking her third cup of tea right now, carefully blowing cold air over it before she takes a sip. We used to work together in the Amerika Haus in Charlottenburg. I worked upstairs in the English teaching section, and she worked downstairs in the library. She is still there, shelving books, helping people with microfilms, answering questions with professional patience. "If I could, I'd move away from here," she says and takes another sip from her tea. "Rather sooner than later." She has brought along a folder full of newspaper clippings, articles about the city that she has carefully dated and puts in front of me like pieces of evidence. There are stories about old restaurants and stores closing down. Stories about pay cuts and rent increases. Stories about name changes for streets and squares (most of them in the east). Stories about the Palast der Republik, whether it should be torn down or left standing, whether it is really full of asbestos, whether its memory is worth anything at all. "I used to read a lot of books," Cornelia says, "but now I mostly read papers." She closes the folder and pushes it toward me. "You can take a look at these, but I'd like them back."

I thank her and slide the folder into my backpack. I think about this: a librarian who no longer reads books. She must have become impatient with them — slow worlds of words that move at a glacial pace compared to the city around her. An hour ago, she told me how she used to organize readings for a library. The readings were always well-attended, and the writers sometimes brought texts that hadn't officially been cleared, hoping to try out uncensored words on an audience that understood the privilege. She never missed any of these readings. It would have been foolish to let them happen without her being there, she said. She needed to know firsthand what was and wasn't read. Someone might have made accusations after the reading, claiming that the words had drifted beyond party truths. She wanted to be prepared for that. And, of course, she also wanted to hear the words in the first place, how they might stray from the mapped-out path and cut into the underbrush. She misses words that can mean with such clarity.

Another train passes overhead, and I shoot another glance at the brick walls. My coffee cup dances on its saucer. "We're not the same," says Cornelia. "We read, talk, and see differently." She says this with so much conviction that I nod before I know whether I agree. "People from the west always think we don't know what's going on. But they're wrong. We had to be good at reading people, trying to figure out whether they could be trusted or not. It's a skill we had to develop." I take a sip from my coffee. I wonder how I have been read for the past three hours. Cornelia orders another cup of tea. "Westerners are so worried about how they come across. It's like being on stage the whole time. You pick whatever act promises the biggest return." She says that it took her a while to figure this out. Years ago, in East Berlin, she saw an American diplomat open a book exhibit at the U.S. embassy. It was a rare occasion. She remembers the room being full of tension; everyone knew that coming to the exhibit was a kind of trespassing that wouldn't go unnoticed. But the American diplomat seemed not to care; he spoke eloquently and moved around the room with sureness, even grace. He didn't pay attention to the traces of fear and hesitation.

He invited everyone to take a look at the books as if it were the most natural of choices. "I admired that man," Cornelia says. "I had never seen anyone act that way. Everything he did looked filled with purpose. He seemed, well . . . he seemed complete — you know, a new kind of man." I listen for a hint of cynicism behind her last words, but there is none. Another train rumbles overhead. "Anyway," she continues, "that was a long time ago. Now I know that this man was nothing special."

When we leave the restaurant, it is dark outside. Cornelia offers to give me a ride to the next U-Bahn station. Her car is parked up the street, a blue Opel Corsa she bought a couple of years ago. It is a small car, the kind that comes in handy in a large city. She tells me that she took some extra driving lessons before she went to the dealer. "To get used to the traffic," she says. She also opted for an automatic transmission. Her friends and family can't get used to the idea of an automatic transmission. They tell her a real car has to be a stick shift, but she has decided to ignore them. She likes not having to worry about a clutch, especially with all the construction going on around the city. When she opens the door for me and I slide into the seat, I notice that the Opel still smells new. There is no clutter at all inside, neither in front nor back. Cornelia fastens her seat belt, turns the key, and the engine springs to life, a distant purr from behind the well-lit dashboard. She puts the car into drive and turns the steering wheel. She checks the side-view mirror, sees no car coming, and steps on the accelerator. Nothing happens. We look at each other, then down at the hand brake. Cornelia giggles as she unlocks it. "You know," she says, her face turned to the roof, "sometimes I sit in this car and I think it's all just like the movies . . . just like the movies."

Sony is convinced that this exciting city will once again play an important role and for that reason has decided to relocate its European headquarters to the German capital. The ultramodern office building will make a significant contribution to Sony's corporate image in the twenty-first century.

On Friedrichstraße, near the new Galeries Lafayette, a tall and slender girl makes her way through the crowd. She carries a sign above her head, which makes her look even taller. This is what the sign says: *Help us greet Arnold Schwarzenegger at 5:30 P.M. on Mohrenstraße*. I check my map.

Mohrenstraße is just a block away, a side street running from east to west. Right now, it is 4:45 P.M. When I get to Mohrenstraße, some forty or fifty people are already waiting outside the new Planet Hollywood restaurant. A small stage has been set up in front of the entrance, framed by two palm trees. The space for the press has been carefully roped off, including a small platform for the photographers and camera operators. I find a place near the back of the crowd, where I climb on top of a fence and watch.

The press section begins to fill. Two camera operators are having an argument about who was there first to claim one of the better spots. Sound systems get checked. At the entrance gate to the press section, two security guards are on duty. They have crew cuts and wear sunglasses. A few Planet Hollywood officials, marked by badges, walk back and forth in front of the stage. One is a young woman dressed in a dark blue suit and platform shoes. She wears a headset, and each time she receives a message from somewhere, she stops and listens, then continues to walk. A man in his midthirties seems to be the supervisor. He wears a loose-fitting gray flannel suit, the kind that almost looks baggy but is really cut with maverick elegance. His blond hair is neatly parted on the left, and his horn-rims lend an air of distinction. The briefcase he carries is old and worn, highlighting the elegant cut of his suit. More and more reporters arrive in front of the stage, among them the well-known news anchor of a breakfast show. People in the crowd begin to point their fingers and whisper.

All of this has been accompanied by dance music flowing from two large speakers. A video screen has been showing movie clips from parties at other Planet Hollywoods. Berlin, I learn, is the thirty-sixth location worldwide. *Planet Hollywood orbits the globe*. At 5:10 P.M. another young woman with a badge climbs onto the stage. Our attention shifts toward her. "I've just received word," she says, "that Arnold is still in the air. But he'll be with us soon." A few shouts and whistles. "And while I'm up here, why don't we practice our welcome for Arnold. As you know, he's an action star. He likes action. I'm sure he wouldn't like a reserved German welcome." More whistles and shouts. "Okay, let's give it a try. I'll count to three, and then we'll all shout 'Arnold.'" She pauses for a moment. "All right, here we go — one, two, three, Arnold." A handful of shouts go up from the crowd. "Is that the best you can do?" the young woman asks. "Come on. Let's hear it for Arnold." Again she begins to count, and again the crowd fails to ignite. "Well, we'll just have to try this again later," she says and walks off the stage.

At 5:30 P.M. the young woman is back. Arnold is still in the air, she tells us. It's going to be 6:00 P.M. before he arrives. She is still worried about the welcome for Arnold and tries once more to warm up the crowd. This time she picks a different chant — "one, two, three, hasta la vista, baby" — and the crowd responds with a little more enthusiasm. At 6:00 P.M. the Planet Hollywood sign on stage collapses and tumbles backward. For a moment, everyone falls silent. We think this is the sign of his arrival, a special effect, but then the support staff races onto the stage and tries to put the sign back up. We realize this isn't part of a plan. At 6:15 P.M. the young woman climbs back on stage. "His plane has landed," she says with a broad smile. "But before he gets here maybe you can help us out. Some of the photographers and cameramen need to leave for other appointments, and they need to have some pictures to take with them. Would you mind applauding as if Arnold had already arrived? Come on, how about it?" Three or four photographers and camera operators get ready for the shot. "One, two, three — go." The crowd gives a mild, uncertain cheer. "A little louder, people, a little louder." The crowd begins to think this is funny. It cheers a little louder. "Just a bit more. I know you can do this." The crowd erupts in front of an empty stage.

Arnold Schwarzenegger arrives at 6:45 P.M.. He is not as tall as I had expected, but everything else looks right: the dark hair, combed straight back; the bushy eyebrows; the massive jaw line above sloping shoulders. He is carrying a large gun, a prop from his latest movie, *Eraser. Eraser — In order to give you a future, he must take away your past.* "This is a Rail Gun," he says. "It has saved my life many times." He speaks German with two accents, one Austrian, the other American. The young woman with the badge is standing next to him, holding a microphone. "Does this kind of gun already exist in reality?" she asks. Arnold Schwarzenegger shakes his head. "No, not yet, but they're working on it." Then he nestles the gun against his body, as if readying himself for enemy fire, and smiles at the press. "It was important to me to open the new Planet Hollywood here in the heart of the new Berlin," he says and smiles. A little later, he thanks us all for coming out.

"Without fans, without the press, there would be no Schwarzenegger." The young woman is impressed with his humility. "Is that an American gesture," she asks, "or is that really Arnold speaking?" He smiles at her. "That is really Arnold."

Inside Cornelia's folder, I find a newspaper article dated August 5, 1996: *But one legacy does bother the Federal Minister for Construction Töpfer significantly, as he points out on the stairs. "This East German smell!" It seems impossible to get rid of. "We have already exchanged some of the carpets, but it doesn't help. The smell must sit inside the walls," complains Töpfer. "I'm usually not like this. But you can imagine that sitting in this smell all day long does dampen one's mood."*

The visiting platform on top of the INFO BOX is open well into the night. I arrive around nine, and take my place in the small line that has formed in front of the gate. There is a turnstile that feeds us one by one to the flight of stairs leading to the roof. The stairs are metal and ring with the sound of our footsteps as we climb. At night, the view from the roof bears no resemblance to what I've seen during the day. All motion has died away — the cranes are frozen at random angles; the dirt roads lie abandoned, day-old diaries of tire tracks; the groundwater lake has flattened out into a silver sheet. There is enough artificial light to see the full size of the site — a valley dotted with backhoes, trucks, generators, water pipes, and the beginnings of new buildings. But the light is uncertain. It leaves enough shadows to blur lines and take away depth, playing tricks with the imagination. Without much effort I can see a change coming over the site.

The new foundations now begin to look old, the ruins of buildings from an earlier age. Now, the purpose isn't construction but excavation, archeology on a grand scale, and the silence in front of me deepens, filling with the slow pace of looking backward. The trucks and backhoes also get caught up in this change. Their oversize wheels and shovels fall out of time and slip beyond their mechanical functions. They are no longer tools but finds themselves, impressive skeletons painstakingly uncovered, their thickness and curvature a matter of curiosity and speculation. The cable drums are deep-sea riddles left by a long-ago ocean; the barges are the hollow carapaces of giant turtles. The site has now become a counterpoint to the city, a passageway into geological time around which the city buzzes like a wound-up toy.

Does your office sometimes remind you of Potsdamer Platz? All of Berlin is a construction site. Your office too? Why don't you talk with Minolta. Our copiers are constructed in a way that requires only a handful of service visits throughout the year. And when our technician comes, he is gone again in no time: Our modular design ensures that everything is taken care of at once.

What has been found underneath Potsdamer Platz:

- Five white porcelain cups
- A Löwenbräu tankard
- Wine glasses
- A Schultheiss beer barrel
- Brown chemists' jars
- An advertisement for a detective agency
- A metal plate with instructions: "First turn on the gas-tap and light all the pilot lights, then cooking can begin."
- Old newspapers
- A 1938 book on the "ABC of Dental Care"
- An octagonal mocha cup
- The remains of a classical column
- A larger-than-life-size head of Apollo

Also:

- Half a multiple rocket launcher
- Bits of grenades and guns
- Melted window glass
- A young soldier's skull protected by a helmet

Whatever you are wanting to arrange, the Potsdamer Platz building site is an extraordinary venue for meetings, lunches, parties, or weddings.

Schönhauser Allee 23–25. On my way north into Prenzlauer Berg, I almost walk right by it. The entrance is a small metal gate under a brick arch. Once I have entered and stand on the other side of the gate, the traffic noise on Schönhauser Allee seems to come from a great distance. The guardhouse is on the right, a tiny structure with small windows. A sign by the door lists opening hours and requests that male visitors enter the cemetery with a head cover. The door to the guardhouse is open, but nobody is sitting at the desk. I knock and wait. A stereo system sits on a shelf behind the desk, a portable TV has found a place on the windowsill. After a minute I knock again, and now I can hear a faint rumble from behind a second door at the back of the room. The groundskeeper seems slightly annoyed by my interruption of whatever he was doing, and I think that not many people must now find their way to this place. I ask for a head cover, and he hands me a blue yarmulke, something I have never worn before and which heightens my sense of being a visitor, of moving among a set of laws I don't know.

The Jewish cemetery on Schönhauser Allee opened in 1827. At that time, my guidebook points out, it lay outside the city limits, which I find hard to believe in light of the five-story apartment buildings that now stand nearby. The cemetery closed in 1880, but a small number of funerals continued into the 1970s. It is difficult to judge the size of the cemetery because of the dense rows of trees. Their leaves connect and form a kind of roof under which the light is sparse and cool, lining the late morning with a hint of dusk. A thick carpet of ivy covers the ground, reaching across gravestones and climbing tree trunks all the way into the branches. The gravestones stand in tight rows, many of them leaning at angles, many tipped over all the way. Snails travel the stones like large dewdrops. I walk deeper into the cemetery and begin to read inscriptions. They are in German and Hebrew. The dates carved into the weathered stones move back and forth between the Jewish and the Christian calendar, rising and falling through the millennia. I turn left and come to the northern wall of the cemetery. Here the graves are larger, more opulent, but they are just as weathered and unkempt. Some of the inscriptions have almost disappeared, leaving an alphabet of broken lines. Behind the wall, not more than a few yards removed, one of the five-story apartment buildings rises up. I wonder about the view one would have from the fourth- or fifth-floor living room windows. Would one be more likely to look out during the summer, when the trees are a solid green cover? Or would the seasons make no difference?

I follow the northern wall for a while and then cut back to the center. A white shimmer appears between the trees that turns out to be a tarp stretched above a large grave. An electric lamp has been fastened underneath the tarp, flooding the gravestone with intense, almost tangible light. A young man wearing a baseball cap hunches over the stone, working at a steady pace. He is surrounded by tools; brushes, scrapers, plastic bottles, and rugs lie scattered at his feet; an air compressor sits on the ground behind him. The stone marks a family grave. It has seven arches cut into it, each framing a name and dates. One of the names is *Max Liebermann (1847–1935)*— the Berlin painter who lived just north of Potsdamer Platz and who began his career with a picture of women plucking geese. In 1933, when his fame had made him honorary president of the Prussian Academy of the Arts, he surrendered his office under increasing political pressure. I can tell without difficulty where the work on the stone has already been finished. It is the fourth arch from the right that lifts away from the others, no longer a sooty gray, but white like chalk. I try to imagine what the stone will look like when the work is done. It will likely be visible from a distance, even on an overcast day and underneath the shadow of trees.

Dear Visitor!
We would be pleased if you could write down your personal vision on this sheet of paper. Afterward you can attach it to our "Vision-Line" in front of the small assembly room. We will publish the results in "Der Tagesspiegel."

1. *The intellectual and emotional state of the republic.*
2. *What virtues do the Germans have to cultivate?*
3. *What values does the country need?*
4. *Your dreams and hopes for Germany.*
5. *The largest danger at the present time?*
6. *What has to be done most urgently?*
7. *Germany's role in Europe and in the world.*

When I meet Mehmet Kalin, he is cleaning the tires of his bicycle. He is standing in front of a small shack whose architecture must violate every city code on the books. I found the shack yesterday walking west on Köpenicker Straße, looking for the place where the Wall used to cut the street in half. There isn't much left to see, no slabs of concrete or watchtower, just a stretch of grass running down a side street. The shack has been built right next to the grass, including a fenced-in garden that sprawls across the former border, filled with regular rows of cabbage. At first sight, the shack looks like a pile of junk without a single straight line. Boards, rafters, car hoods, sheets of tin, bricks, and plastic tarps have been pushed together into the faint echo of a house. The fence around the garden shows the same workmanship — wire mesh, rusted garden gates, boards, and mattress springs encircle the cabbage.

I walk up to Mehmet Kalin and introduce myself. I tell him that I discovered the shack yesterday and that I'm curious to find out what it is doing here. He doesn't seem to mind my question. He asks me to wait a moment while he locks away the bicycle and then suggests we talk inside the shack, where we can sit down. The door is low and narrow, and I have to bend my head to be able to slip inside. Instead of a room, I now find myself in a kind of passageway that leads past a small enclosure on the right (in the half-light I can see old suitcases, a pile of coats, an overturned oven, a guitar without strings) and an open vista of the garden on the left. We are walking on a set of planks, which bounce with every step, keeping us a few inches above the cabbage. Then comes a sharp 180-degree turn and a short flight of stairs. Here the walls move in close enough to make us turn sideways as we begin to climb. At the top of the stairs, we turn left and enter a low, square room full of daylight that comes in through the plastic tarp roof. Mehmet Kalin offers me an old desk chair, while he sits down on a stool next to a woodstove. There are no other chairs, but the floor has been covered with blankets, sheepskins, and pieces of Styrofoam. A scratched slice of mirror hangs on the back wall, framed by two handsaws.

"My father started this garden," Mehmet Kalin says. "He stopped working in 1985, and he didn't know what to do with his time. He had worked construction . . . hard work, you know, and going to the mosque to pray wasn't enough to fill his days." His voice is soft as he talks about his father, his German woven around a Turkish accent. But I can also hear Berlin in his sentences, hard-nosed consonants that tell of the years he has spent in the city. His father arrived in Germany in 1964 to find work. Back then, Mehmet Kalin was two years old, which means he has lived in this country for thirty-two years, much longer than I have. I want to know whether anybody complained about the garden when it started up. Could an old Turkish man simply walk up to the Wall and start planting vegetables? Mehmet Kalin laughs quietly. "Oh yes, the police told my father several times to stop, but he never did. Once a policeman tried to keep my father from getting water from a public pipeline not far from here. They wrestled over the valve until it burst open by accident, and sprayed them until they were soaked." We both laugh. I imagine Mehmet Kalin's father and the police officer embracing in a half-serious struggle, two unlikely dancers, pushing each other until the water has cooled them off.

"There was one other time," Mehmet Kalin says. "My father was in the garden and heard a voice behind him. He turned around and saw three East German soldiers looking over the Wall. They must have used ladders or something. They told my father that his garden couldn't be here. They told him it was a security risk." I imagine this too: Three East German soldiers, cut off above the waist, leaning into West Germany, concerned about vegetables. "What happened?" I ask. "Did they do anything?" Mehmet Kalin shakes his head. "No, nothing happened. My father just kept gardening."

A light rain has begun to fall and taps the plastic roof. Mehmet Kalin plays with the drawstring of his coat, twirling it around his index finger, a small propeller that shrinks and grows. I can hear footsteps coming up the stairs, and a moment later an old Turkish woman enters the room. She wears a traditional head scarf and a black coat buttoned all the way to the top. Mehmet Kalin addresses her in Turkish, and she bends down to the stove, filling it with wood and paper. After she has lit the stove, she pushes together a couple of sheepskins and settles on the floor. A piece of Styrofoam serves her as a backrest. I ask Mehmet Kalin what he does for a living, and he tells me that he is a bricklayer, working construction like his father. He has worked all over the city, even, for a little while, at Potsdamer Platz. "I took my whole family to see Potsdamer Platz," he says. "We took pictures. Potsdamer Platz very good, you know, very good for Germany's future." I want to know whether he still thinks about going back to Turkey some day. He isn't sure. His children speak German now, and for the most part he likes it here. "Only right after the changes," he adds, "when the Wall came down, it was a difficult time. With all the violence that happened, I was worried for my children. I thought all the time, what if someone tries to hurt them on their way to school. If someone hurts me, I can fight, you know. Then I will die or he. But my children can't do that. Back then, I was very worried."

The rain falls harder now, collecting in small puddles on top of the tarp. The old woman speaks a few Turkish words, and Mehmet Kalin shakes his head; he looks out the window into the garden, where the cabbage leaves dip up and down in rhythm with the drops. "You know," he says, "there is a map of this part of the city. I've seen it. And my father's garden is on it. It says *small Turkish garden*, right there on the map."

Central Berlin lies in an ice-age glacial valley with a range of deposits; this means that building in Berlin is by no means straightforward.

I didn't expect to find divers at the construction site. They work on a square pontoon, a crew of three, one of whom descends into the brownish water, while the other two stand watch and feed the braided oxygen and radio lines after him. The water is too dirty for the diver to see once his lead weights have pulled him to a depth of twenty meters. Down at the bottom, his work is a mix of touch and spatial memory. Like a blind man, he fingers the cement blocks that will soon carry a building. I wonder what he can hear down there besides the radio voice channeled into the helmet. Maybe the engine noise from above travels this far. Maybe he is surrounded by complete silence that sometimes makes him forget where he is.

When the diver comes back to the surface, gravity catches up with him, and he climbs onto the pontoon with the awkward hobble of a seal gaining land. His two partners are there to help him, lifting him to his feet and keeping an eye on the tangle of hoses. They are dressed casually, wearing t-shirts, jeans, and fatigues. First they unscrew the diver's helmet, then they take off his lead weights. They chat and joke with each other as the diver peels himself out of his suit. They don't look like construction specialists, men who have to worry about keeping schedules and measure their tasks in centimeters. Set off by themselves, floating on a pontoon scattered with diving suits, oxygen tanks, ropes, cables, buckets, they look like a band of adventurers, men who dive for the stuff of stories — gold, silver, the hidden secrets of sunken ships. . . .

magnificent relics from the emperor's era to be integrated into the new building
gleaming with black granite
the way to a golden future
unimaginable quality
a striking sign
spectacular
legendary
colossal

At the south end of Friedrichstraße, not far from the old Checkpoint Charlie, I finally decide to put my hand against one of the pink and blue water lines. I want to know whether I can feel the rush of water on the inside or maybe the faint buzz of a pump working. The metal pipe is solid and cool and still. It looks like an elaborate, mile-long statue. A soccer ball flies up from behind the next house corner, arches over the pipe a few yards in front of me, and bounces into the middle of the street. A second later, a boy comes chasing after the ball. He checks for traffic with a quick turn of his head, runs out into the street, snatches the ball, and is gone again. When I reach the house corner, I find a small playground wedged between the five-story buildings. The boy and a friend are kicking the ball back and forth across a couple of benches. They are concentrating hard, keeping their eyes on the ball, their bodies in constant motion. They are keeping score and right now have no attention left for anything else.

I watch them for a couple of minutes and listen as the score climbs through the rapid pulse of their breathing. Only when the ball bounces off into some bushes and stops the game do they notice me. "Hi," I say, "what are you playing?" The taller of the two boys has picked up the ball and now holds it casually at his side. "It's just something we made up," he says, "kind of a mix between tennis and soccer." He wears thin wire-rim glasses, and the first shadow of a beard curves above his upper lip. His name is Christoph. His friend, Jan, is a full head shorter, no trace of a beard. "We aren't really supposed to be here," Christoph says. "Our school doesn't like it when we sneak away during breaks." Both Christoph and Jan grew up not far from here, in the old heart of the city. I ask what they remember of East Germany. They shrug their shoulders at the same time. "Not much," Jan says.

"Guess I remember the pioneer meetings at school in the morning. We had to wear a red scarf and stuff. Some of it was fun."

Jan was nine when the Wall came down, Christoph was ten. "Man, you wouldn't believe how many people showed up at our apartment that night," Christoph says. "Our place was packed with friends and family, everyone talking at once." The first thing Christoph did after that night was to go over into West Berlin and buy a remote control buggy. "Pretty strange if you think about it," he says, "but I only had this plastic tank to play with. It had a battery cable, and all you could do was run after it — that thing bored me to tears." Jan doesn't recall what he did back then. But he likes the changes. "Always something happening, something to see." For a while, he had to find a new way to school every day because of the construction. "It was kind of cool," he says and sounds pleased to live in a city that plays tricks on him, that reshuffles its streets overnight like a stack of cards.

Christoph and Jan both like to go over into the western half. They like to shop on Kurfürstendamm, where the stores are close together. Do they ever feel out of place on Kurfürstendamm? Do people strike them as different? They think about this for a second, then Jan shakes his head. "No, can't say I've noticed that." Christoph bounces the ball once. He looks ready to return to the game. "Here's how I see it," he says. "I know some really stupid Westerners. But I also know some really stupid Easterners. I don't see the big difference." Then he bounces the ball again and turns to Jan. "You ready?" "Sure." We say good-bye. I see Jan make the first kick, sending the ball high across the benches. Christoph has been ready for a while, watching the ball come toward him, his lanky body curved like a bow.

In principle, every second Berliner can imagine moving to the other half of the city: 46 percent of West Berliners and 56 percent of East Berliners. In reality, only 2 percent of West and East Berliners have made the move so far.

On my last day I borrow a car from a friend. I drive in a southeasterly direction, rolling through Mitte, Treptow, and Schöneweide. When I reach Köpenick, I take a wrong turn and end up in a maze of narrow streets. For a while I travel in circles, until I find a way to reconnect to my original route. Trams are still running in this part of the city. Their overhead wires stretch above like a gossamer roof. Once I have passed

Müggelheim, I start looking for a small asphalt road on my right. According to the article I found in the newspaper two days ago, the road should link up to a short trail, which in turn should lead me to a clearing in the woods. And in that clearing I should find a hill — two meters high and forty meters long — under which Lenin lies buried. These are the remains not of the real man but of his granite counterpart, a nineteen-meter-high statue that used to raise its fist in the eastern neighborhood of Friedrichshain.

After another five minutes of driving through pine forest, I find the asphalt road and follow it to the trailhead. There is a large ranger station at the start of the trail, and I stop to ask for directions. The station sits behind a high fence, which has several Beware of Dog signs attached to it. I walk up to the gate, find the doorbell, and wait for someone to come out. A door opens and the first one to appear is an Irish setter who trots to the gate at a leisurely pace, sits down, and watches me. Next is a man in his forties with dark hair and a mustache. He too seems in no hurry to make it to the gate, and I worry that I may have woken him from a slumber, which wouldn't help his mood. "Yes?" the man asks as he steps next to the dog. "I'm sorry to disturb you," I say. "I was just wondering whether this trail might take me to the clearing in which the Lenin statue lies buried?" The man doesn't answer right away. He bends down to the dog and pats it. "The Lenin statue? Yes, that's down there, about four hundred meters from here." He doesn't sound particularly annoyed, and I try another question. "Were you here when they brought the statue? I mean did you see them deliver it?" He nods. "It arrived in the evening, loaded onto several trucks. They had cut it up into 125 pieces, all neatly numbered. Since then we've had a few people sneak out there, trying to dig it up with shovels. But the pieces are way too heavy for that." I thank him for his help, and he turns back to the house. I start down the trail.

The clearing turns out to be a small valley, crisscrossed by sandy hills. Much of the ground is covered by knee-high grass, and right away I know that I won't be able to tell where the statue lies. The hills look too similar, their dimensions hard to gauge under open sky. I climb two or three of them and dig up some of the sand with my heel, but no granite finger or eyebrow comes to the surface. I would like to know how deeply those 125 pieces lie buried, whether a rainy summer could wash them back into visibility. And I also would like to know whether the pieces are arranged in order, still suggesting the shape of a man. Maybe the city workers unloaded the pieces at random, a foot next to a chin, a knee above a shoulder, a head below a neck — a puzzle of granite anatomy left for someone else to figure out.

From the hill I stand on, I can overlook the entire clearing. A slight breeze has sprung up and bends the grass in front of me. I can hear the breeze moving through the branches of the nearby pines, and for a moment I think it is the only noise. But then I hear the faint traces of traffic coming out of the northwest, the stop and go of engines climbing through gears.

Apprenticeship

I hadn't expected that planning my wedding would involve the question of how to light a barn. But in the weeks before the wedding, Karen and I kept loading up our car with clamp lamps, light bulbs, extension cords, and duct tape, and we would drive the twelve miles between our apartment in Iowa City and the barn outside Downey. We usually left at dusk and arrived just in time to see the red of the barn fade between the surrounding oaks. We would push open the large sliding door and climb the stairs to the hayloft, where we spread out everything we had brought in neat piles. Much of our work had to be done with a ladder, and some of it at a considerable height. Right from the start, Karen made it clear that the ladder would be my responsibility. She volunteered to hold it in place, but she would have nothing to do with climbing it. I didn't mind this arrangement at first. However, I soon discovered what it felt like to be near the top of the ladder, ten feet above the floor, both hands sticking to duct tape. It scared me. And the more nervous I became, the more often I reminded Karen to hold on to the ladder. With each reminder, she grew a little more impatient, telling me to stop worrying and finish up. It didn't help our mood that the hayloft was usually hot and humid, and before long we let our voices get louder and edgier — each of us eager to ignore the other but unable to do so, kept in place by the ladder and the job at hand.

I had found the barn a year earlier with the help of a friend who took me to see it on a fall Sunday, and after a few minutes of roaming the place, I knew it would be right for the reception. I called Karen that night and told her what I had seen — a red octagonal barn, 114 years old, with a hayloft that felt like a cathedral. I didn't say much about the fist-sized holes in the floor, or the bulging walls, or the stack of rotting hay bales. While I ran through my description on the phone, Karen listened patiently. I told her that the barn had been bought by a professor in town, who had been fixing it up for several years. He had even put in two simple restrooms, a fact I emphasized, sounding as upbeat as a travel agent about an ocean view. She said she wanted to see pictures to make up her mind, but I could tell that she liked the idea.

Karen and I had met in Iowa four years earlier, and we had talked about finding a reception place that would somehow acknowledge that fact. It was a bit of nostalgia we thought we deserved, in part because we hadn't had much time together. Shortly after we met, Karen left for California to continue with graduate school, while I had my own degree to finish in Iowa. From then on we mostly knew each other as voices on the phone, running up our bills, gauging each other's moods, trading our days in installments.

Three months after my phone call about the barn, Karen came to visit for Christmas. As I had hoped, she ended up as enthusiastic about the place as I was. She was more critical about the obvious shortcomings — holes in the floor, primitive restrooms, plenty of places for kids to get into trouble — but it wasn't enough to deter her. After our inspection, we went back to the apartment and jotted down all we needed to do to put the wedding together by next September. We wrote without pause and without order, as if trying to catch up with our own courage. We listed table decorations next to Bible verses next to motels, and afterward started in on the guest list, jumping back and forth between America and Germany. Even on paper, it looked like a daunting task.

I had taken some time to get up my courage to ask Karen to marry me. My hesitation had nothing to do with what I felt. I knew that I loved Karen. Her generosity, her quick laughter, the way she listened to others with interest and care, as if there could be no question that all of it should matter. It was something else I found more difficult to figure out. If Karen and I got married, we would make a commitment to pull together not only the strands of two lives, but also those of two countries, Germany and America — two sets of coordinates that might never add up to a single map.

Even before I started looking for an engagement ring, I had decided to return to Germany after finishing school. I had spent eight of the last ten years in America, which made the country feel real and my place in it no longer arbitrary. And yet I wanted to go back. It was a gut decision that refused to be unraveled by logic. Maybe it was nostalgia again, the kind of romantic projection distance makes possible. Maybe it was more. Over the past year I had begun to think of my family in Hamburg with fresh intensity, memories floating up like air trapped under water. I thought of my father pulling the door of our apartment shut at 4:30 in the morning on his way to work. My brother painting his red Citroën with blazing yellow birds. My mother counting her birthday cards each March and announcing the result over dinner. I worried that their lives had become a series of snapshots, albums to open and update once a year or less. Occasionally, I caught myself imagining my life in America years from now, when I might be a father watching his son or daughter grow into an American childhood, as if there could be no other. I even imagined myself a grandfather whose family, coming together for Thanksgiving, would urge the immigrant to tell stories from the country he had left. And I would oblige, surprised by the faces around the table, handing out words with the faintest trace of an accent.

I understood that a lot of these thoughts were lazy and sentimental. But they still brought me up hard against the idea of becoming an immigrant, an idea that didn't want to fit. I had been a foreign student up to this point, who could think of his time in America as temporary, an extended immersion in another culture that would leave its traces, a second rhythm playing off the first, but that wouldn't require real sacrifice. If I stayed, I knew this version of things would become less true with each year. To stay would mean accepting that my story would, in some way, start over, and I would have to let go of the certainty that comes from being known over time. To immigrate means the willingness to be visible and invisible at the same time, a doubling of the self that is both exciting and exhausting, both gain and loss, and no matter how I turned this thought in my head, it was the loss I couldn't get around.

I didn't try to keep this from Karen. We talked about it openly, and she surprised me. If I had to return to Germany, she said, it wouldn't make a difference to her. She didn't feel rooted in America the way I seemed to be in Germany. Maybe, she said, it had something to do with her family moving when she was young, her father, a professor, taking jobs in Illinois, Texas, and then, the biggest change for them all, Alaska. What mattered to her most was that we would be in one place.

I hadn't expected that kind of sureness. And even after she had told me, I found it hard to trust. Maybe she could be so sure because she had never lived abroad for more than a few months. What if living in Germany didn't add up to something that could contain her? What if it left her unsettled, spread thin, the days only increasing her desire to return? I worried we would have no chance under such circumstances. But in the midst of that downward spiral, I could catch myself by remembering something else Karen had said. She, too, was afraid of becoming invisible, she said, but she trusted that we could push against that fear. If my years in America had helped me understand who she was, then why shouldn't her years in Germany give her a better understanding of me? In the end, she said, we might find that how we take shape together over the slow span of years will outweigh the question of where to live. The more I thought about this — still wary of the ease and symmetry of her suggestion — the more ground it gave me to stand on, until, with my heart racing, I stopped once more at the jeweler and bought the ring I thought she'd like.

A week after Karen had seen the barn for the first time, her parents came to join us from New York. They were eager to learn more about our plans, and they were also eager to contribute. Karen was their only daughter, the youngest of three children, and her wedding wasn't going to be a haphazard affair. I had sent a carefully worded card to Karen's parents after our engagement, thanking them for the hospitality they had shown me. I wrote that the marriage would bring changes for all of us and that I was looking forward to our sharing of thoughts as we planned the wedding. Her father had written back right away, a friendly e-mail expressing his pleasure. Her mother, who had been away on a trip, didn't write back for several weeks. When her card arrived, it expressed pleasure as well, but it also spoke of high standards and suggested I live up to them. All in all, Karen's parents and I hadn't spent a lot of time around each other — a few short weekends filled with courtesy and dinners. Even after four years of dating Karen, I still addressed her parents as Mr. and Mrs. Bergquist and, for the most part, didn't mind the rituals that governed our meetings. Now, those rituals would no longer do, and I had no idea yet what should take their place.

Things didn't get off to a good start. The four of us drove out to the barn early in the morning. The temperature had dropped to just above zero, and the wind kept whipping fresh snow across the road. When we pulled up in front of the barn, we could hear the snow crunching under our tires. The sound made my heart sink. It looked as if this visit would do little to sell Karen's parents on our choice of location. The owner of the barn, who had agreed to meet us for a brief tour, had already arrived. He waved from the hayloft and told us to come up. An old stereo, which he kept hooked up near the stairs, was booming classical music through the crisp morning air, sounding entirely implausible. We all shook hands and then followed the owner around the loft as he explained to us about the laminated beams holding up the barn. There were eight of them, he told us, each one made up of eighteen strips of wood carefully soaked and curved, each one running from the base of the loft to the roof's apex, all of it, he said, an architectural feat that had few counterparts in its day. Karen and I kept glancing at each other and then at her parents, wondering how they liked what they saw. It didn't look promising. Her mother held on to a large file folder — a collection of ideas for our wedding — and each step she took looked measured and deliberate, as if she expected the boards to give and send her down to the threshing floor. Karen's father carried a camera and kept taking pictures from different angles, looking as solemn as an insurance agent shooting water damage. And I had to agree that the place looked less inviting than it had before. Some birds had taken refuge in the cupola, from where they had sent their droppings all over the hayloft. Snow had blown in through the cracks, fanning out from the walls like spilled sugar, and a couple of times a gust caught us with such strength that it was hard to know whether we were inside at all.

There was little talk on the way back to the house. We sat down in the living room and, after another round of silence, began to compare notes. Karen's parents had more than a few reservations. They wanted to know what we planned to do in case our wedding day turned out to be too hot or cold. What if it rained and the grass in front of the barn turned into a mud hole? They worried about the comfort of our older guests, and they wondered what kind of caterer would take on a place like this — out in the country, dirty, no kitchen, no hot water. Then Mrs. Bergquist said she had one other question to ask. Were we planning to serve alcohol at this wedding? She looked at Karen, who didn't answer right away. Karen and I had talked about this before, not at great length, but we had decided to have champagne and wine at the reception. She had told me that her parents wouldn't be thrilled, but it hadn't sounded like much of a problem. "Yes," Karen said. I looked over at Mrs. Bergquist. She had turned her head toward the window. It took me several seconds to realize that she had begun crying. Nobody spoke. I tried to think of something to say, but couldn't. Finally, Mrs. Bergquist took out a Kleenex, and somehow that small gesture gave us all a reason to stir, pushing words back into reach. "Well, you know . . . maybe Karen and I can think about this some more," I said, and for the rest of the day and the next, as we checked out local photographers — looking at pictures of couples standing near placid lakes, sitting in sporty convertibles, and walking in the purple haze of ocean sundowns — nothing further was said. Our conversation moved on to other topics, staying on safer ground, our words pleasant and polite, but alert.

In the end, we gave up on the alcohol. Karen's parents didn't want to host a reception where champagne and wine would be served. They suggested a kind of coffee hour after the church ceremony, leaving the barn party to us and our friends. It was a fair compromise, but it still felt like a wedge pushed into our wedding day — two receptions instead of one, splintering the fellowship that we wanted for that particular day. Even after we had made the decision, I kept trying to understand how it had happened. For days, I kept rearranging the few bits and pieces I knew about Mrs. Bergquist, hoping to catch a glimpse of what she might be seeing. I knew she had grown up in Los Angeles in the 1940s and 1950s, a Baptist family of Swedish descent, her father a skilled carpenter who had built the house they lived in. Church was important, Karen said, and so were the rules about movies, dance, and drink. Much later, at college in Sacramento, she earned a degree in home economics, taught for a while, then focused on her own family when she got married and the children started coming. I knew that she still ran her kitchen with an expert's passion. She was an excellent cook, and when she was busy preparing meals, this much I had learned, it was smart not to get in her way. The care she took with food was the same kind she took in all matters of family. She usually knew who was doing what, and any kind of change — a new job, a trip, a sudden illness—was carefully considered and, if necessary, followed by a trip to the public library to find out what such an event might mean. The line she drew around her family, it seemed, was clear and strong, a kind of threshold from which she could study the outside and on which I had now arrived, asking to be let in.

I called my father in Hamburg a few days after the Bergquists had visited. When he heard about the alcohol, he fell silent for so long that I thought our connection had been cut. "Whose wedding is this anyway?" he finally asked, giving me his answer along with his question. I knew, of course, why he sounded surprised. For almost a hundred years my family has been making a living selling beer and beverages in Hamburg. For four generations we have delivered drinks to stores, restaurants, bars, and cafeterias. It is a tradition that fills my father with pride, and the alcohol, for him, is just a small ordinary part of it all — a product to be bought from the breweries, priced, sold, sometimes enjoyed. And there was one other reason, I thought, why my father was staying silent, waiting for me to make him understand. In my family, and in the families of the friends I had grown up with, religious rules belonged to the quaint atmosphere of Christmas and Easter, something we approved of like the fine workmanship that had gone into our holiday decorations, something to fold up when the time came and drop into a drawer. I had grown up among lukewarm Lutherans in a city that has always been more interested in the pragmatics of trade than in matters of the spirit. "It's hard to explain, Dad," I mumbled into the receiver and then added something large and fuzzy about different traditions and the need for respect.

After I had hung up, I began to wonder how my friends in Hamburg would take this news about a dry reception. I wondered whether they would, as they had done on occasion, look mildly incredulous about this country I had moved to. Several of them travel to America regularly, and after their return we talk about what they have seen and heard. They say that the size of the country never ceases to surprise them. They talk about the solitude that is possible here. They note the speed with which conversations among strangers can excavate the personal. In the afterglow of their trips, they find it easy to hold up America between two fingers, turning it like a coin and telling me its value. Sometimes they surprise me with their sharp summaries that catch what I, too, find to be true. But just as often they seem to be talking about another country entirely, and then I disagree and give them my own quick analysis. Other times, however, I just listen to their version of things, while my mind fills with faces, words, houses, meals, the wooded shoreline of a lake. And no matter how much I try to see patterns in those moments, all I find are the days lived in a country I know well enough to lose sight of.

Before returning to New York, Mrs. Bergquist had left us the black file folder filled with wedding ideas. She had done a good bit of research via the Internet, and as Karen and I fingered our way through the alphabetical pockets, we found address lists for local caterers and florists, pictures of wedding receptions, and sample texts for wedding invitations, the kind that speak of "honour" and spell out the date of the occasion with medieval clarity. The folder was massive, and it made our own list of things to do look like the work of amateurs. After a few days of exploring the folder, Karen found a single yellow sheet torn from a legal pad. She looked it over quietly, then gave it to me. The page was filled with Mrs. Bergquist's handwriting both on the printed lines and in the margins. I started reading, and right away the words looked familiar. It was the text of the card I had written to the Bergquists months earlier, shortly after the engagement. Line by line Mrs. Bergquist had copied my words and put her own next to them. Most of what she had written were questions. What is he saying? What is he offering? What is he expecting from us?

My first reaction was disbelief. I asked Karen what she thought this was about. She shrugged her shoulders. "I don't know." All I could do was look back at the sheet, my words and Mrs. Bergquist's together on one page. I was angry, because at that moment it seemed clear that the sheet was a sign of distrust, letting me know that I wasn't the ideal candidate she had in mind. Her scrutiny of my words made them feel false and hypocritical, as if, like the villain of a novel, I was about to ruin Karen and make off with her jewelry. I was angry enough to pace the living room, murmuring to myself and calling up images of friends who, in some imaginary courtroom, were falling all over each other to testify to the integrity of my character. I also thought of my parents, whose support I didn't have to earn and whose ways, which can drive me to despair on a normal day, I now claimed with tribal fury. If Mrs. Bergquist couldn't see who I was, other people could.

I read the sheet again the next day. This time in a more reasonable state. I followed my own sentences written out in Mrs. Bergquist's handwriting and afterward studied her words in the margins, not as judgments but as questions. What is he saying? What is he offering to do? What is he expecting from us? Mrs. Bergquist was considering what I had written. It had taken me a long time to compose those lines, and now she was taking a long time weighing them. I had to admit the balance of it made sense.

And like Mrs. Bergquist, I had questions of my own. There was, for example, the ongoing surprise to see Karen's and my decision to marry take shape in small, ordinary steps. Even my final trip to the jeweler, the one I had expected to stand out and quiet the rush of thoughts in my head, ended up being entirely comprehensible. The glass door with opening hours, the long old-fashioned counter, behind it the saleswoman with an eager smile under too much makeup. The small gray box that slipped into my jacket — no weight at all — and back outside, the traffic still moving at the same pace, the two businessmen still talking at the corner. Maybe this was what my card had felt like to Mrs. Bergquist. A thing so real on her dining room table, next to the morning paper, that it couldn't have anything to do with her daughter getting married. She must have celebrated her daughter's wedding more than once in her mind, and each time it must have been flawless. Now, like all of us, she had to find a way of letting in reality, and part of that task, for her, involved figuring out who I was — a man of thirty-three who had spent a few nights at her house, praised her food, and who, if she had pieced together the whole picture, was about to ask her daughter to live abroad. Maybe she wanted me to find the sheet to let me know she was anxious. If that was her intention, I could understand it. Maybe I could even be grateful for it, because I, too, was afraid, wanting to be sure that what Karen and I were doing would turn out right.

Over the next few months, Karen visited me in Iowa whenever she could, and we started working our way down the list of things to do. We found some sparkling cider that we tried with dinner for a few days, swishing it around in our mouths like wine connoisseurs, then declared it good enough for the reception. We hooked up with a caterer, a small, fast-spoken chef with an Italian name, who had been recommended by a friend. He told us that the Midwest was in the midst of a food Renaissance and that we had nothing to worry about. He aimed at perfection, he said, explosions of flavor that would be remembered. We also settled on a local band whose music we had liked for a long time. We owned a couple of their CDs and played them in our kitchen late at night. Mostly, we tried two-stepping, tables and chairs pushed to the side. But even that simple step gave me problems. While Karen glided with the beat, I counted out loud, keeping my eyes on the refrigerator.

Our lighting trips to the barn started in August. By then, Karen had finished her coursework out west and moved back to Iowa. The first few times we showed up at the barn, we didn't get much accomplished at all. We had no sense of the space yet, and the few clamp lamps we brought along only cut the darkness into random patterns. Gradually, loading up on more lamps, more extension cords, and more duct tape, we figured out where to place the lights and at what angle. About ten days before the ceremony, we hit upon the setup we wanted. That night, we were hot and tired, and our patience had worn thin again from wrestling with the ladder. When I plugged in the last lamp, completing the blanket of light against the ceiling, we stood next to each other, silent. There was enough light to show the extent of the roof, the curve of the laminated beams, and the reverse ladder leading to the cupola. Enough light to see the patched-up floorboards and the tall hay-chutes, which now looked like another set of ladders ending in midair. We kept standing in the center of the hayloft for a good long time. We let our eyes travel across the ceiling, down along the beams, across the floor, and then all the way up into the cupola, looking, I imagine, like apprentice acrobats waiting for the audience to arrive.

My parents flew into town a week before the wedding. Mr. and Mrs. Bergquist arrived a day later. We had decided to let the first meeting take place at Bill Zuber's family restaurant. It's a tourist place outside of town, part of a nineteenth-century German settlement, and it celebrates its ethnic heritage with a vengeance. Checkered tablecloths, waitresses decked out in dirndls, bratwurst and schnitzel and sauerkraut on the menu. The food is decent, though, and it's served family style — we figured that conversation might be helped by dishes being passed back and forth.

It was a good move. Everyone arrived on time, dressed casually but with the kind of care you reserve for first encounters. The food came quickly, no unnecessary pauses, and Karen and I settled into our role as interpreters, translating between bites of cottage cheese and corn. Mrs. Bergquist surprised my mother and the rest of the table by asking for the potatoes in German. "Very good," my mother answered in English. She was suddenly inspired and willing to try out the few English words she remembers from a long-ago class. With bowls of food keeping our hands busy, conversation did turn out to be easy. Polite questions about life in New York and Hamburg, German recipes, and the inconveniences of air travel. Nobody mentioned the wedding, as if we all had signed an agreement to leave that topic for later.

That night at Bill Zuber's I was pleased to see my mother relax. I knew she wasn't particularly fond of coming to America. She misses the rituals of her daily routines in Hamburg — the drawn-out shopping trips with her bicycle, the chats with neighbors, her afternoon coffee, which she celebrates like a high mass, and the string of early evening phone calls to friends, rewinding the day and everything it brought. My mother loves conversation, even though she hardly ever talks about the things that make her restless and afraid. In America she has to let go of conversation. She ends up having to watch from the outside, and the country she sees, for the most part, she finds hard to understand. That night at Bill Zuber's, however, I didn't see her hesitate. She was having a good time, praising the food in English — "I like. It's very fine." — and I was amazed to realize that the restaurant Karen and I had chosen partly tongue-in-cheek put my mother at ease. In this happy, strange place with its misspelled German menu, my mother felt less cut loose; it helped her to anchor herself and sort out the emotions that came with sitting next to her son and his future wife and in-laws, a homemaker and an education professor from a place called Long Island, two people her age with whom she would likely never be able to talk one-on-one.

After dinner I took my parents back to the hotel. My mother wanted me to ask the receptionist for another room. The one they had slept in the night before had no windows to open, just a big air conditioner with too many switches and incomprehensible instructions. I should have remembered this. My mother dislikes rooms that are closed off. At home, she always sleeps with the window open, praising fresh air as if it were a kind of vitamin that can prevent colds and a slew of other diseases. The hotel clerk had another room available, one with a sliding window, and as soon as we had moved the luggage, my mother pulled the curtain aside and opened the window all the way.

The next day over breakfast, she told me that students started singing outside the window at one in the morning. "They had instruments," my mother said, "tubas and drums. They were dancing in the fountain and singing and laughing. It was so loud." I explained to her that what she saw was part of the big football weekend, the two state teams celebrating their rivalry, which can turn this small town upside down. "Is that what it was," my mother said without really listening to my explanation. She simply continued describing what she saw, the bodies and the dancing, not sounding angry at all about losing sleep. "Dancing in the fountain. Can you imagine?" she said and glanced at my father as if to recruit a witness to this outrageous spectacle. I laughed, thinking I had caught her again at a loss about America. But then she said, "They looked so young dancing like that . . . just very young," and I couldn't tell anymore whether she was talking about something she had never seen or something she remembered well.

My parents and the Bergquists didn't see much more of each other during the week before the wedding. Karen and her family, which now included her grandmother and aunt, who had arrived from California, stayed busy wrapping gifts for the rehearsal dinner, tying cloth napkins with sprigs of southernwood, and folding parchment paper into cones to be filled with birdseed that was supposed to rain down on us next Saturday. It was a dizzying number of details to keep track of. Each night Karen told me how things were coming along, checking off items on our list with obvious pleasure. My task was to get the barn in shape. I took my parents out to the place early in the week to let them have a first look and make my own list of what was left to do. "This is it," I said as we pulled up in front of the barn. We pushed open the sliding door and stepped inside. "Oh," my mother said, wanting to hide her shock, but failing completely. "Rustic . . . , isn't it?" My father didn't say anything. He walked a bit further into the barn and rapped his knuckles against one of the beams. "Solid," he said.

The main project I had left to finish was to fill in the holes in the hayloft floor. They weren't overly large, but big enough to catch a heel or swallow the leg of a chair, which, Karen had said, wasn't going to happen at our reception. My father volunteered to pitch in right away, and I was glad to have some help. We started work the next morning while it was still cool, dragging pieces of leftover lumber to the hayloft and setting out the tools we would need. The owner of the barn had given us the key to his toolshed, and everything we needed was there — power drill, electric saw, and as many wood screws as we could want. "What do you want me to do?" my father asked after we had finished setting up. I told him to measure a few holes so I could start cutting the wood. We soon found our rhythm, working straight through lunch and into the afternoon. By three o'clock the heat up in the hayloft was almost unbearable. I kept looking over at my father to see how he was taking it. His heart puts out only half of what it should, damaged from years of working too much in the family business. On hot days his blood pressure can drop like a stone, blurring his vision and slipping him next to unconsciousness.

"Ready for a break, Dad?" He nodded and pushed himself up from the floor. "You're the boss," he said, wiping off his face with the sleeve of his shirt. We stopped for twenty minutes, drinking water and feeling too tired to talk. Then we put in another hour, and as he had done all afternoon, my father worked quickly and consistently, eager to anticipate anything I might ask, holding down the wood when I worked the saw and praising the precision of my cuts. He laid out the screws according to size. He kept the power cord from getting tangled. He brushed away the sawdust. A couple of times he tried to guess which piece of wood I would pick up next, and we both bent down at the same time and bumped against each other. "Oh, Entschuldigung," my father would say and take a few steps back, waiting until I had finished setting up. Then he stood next to me again, keeping an eye on the power cord, lining up the screws, praising my cuts.

On the way back to town, we rolled down the windows and tried to cool off in the breeze. I thanked my father for his help. "Don't mention it," he said and kept looking outside at the fields rushing by. I tried to think of something else to say to keep us from staying silent. My father and I don't manage conversations too well. We get derailed by the things we should talk about but can't quite put into words. Instead, we find other topics, innocent ground that can still turn soft in a matter of seconds. One of the things we talk about is America. My father loves coming to America. He admires almost everything the country puts in front of him — clean parks and shopping malls, the overwhelming friendliness of Midwesterners, stores that never close and highways that sneak up to the horizon. What he doesn't see, or doesn't want to see, are the things that aren't that picture perfect. He marvels at all the bustle around him, which he reads as proof that this is a country of people who do and not just talk. At the heart of America he finds what he respects the most — an old-fashioned work ethic that promises redemption and clarity of purpose in return for self-reliance and exhaustion. I can hear it play like a familiar tune behind his exclamations over the size of buildings and fields and neon-crazed strip malls. Once he gets going like this, it doesn't take long until he brings up Germany in comparison and makes it sound like a backward, self-pitying island of bureaucrats. I know he is venting his frustrations built up from years of running a business in the midst of what he thinks of as too many regulations, too many fees and taxes, too many people getting by on a free ride. Whenever my father falls into his American rapture, I roll with it for a bit. Then I talk back.

The more my father praises what he sees, the more I try to prove him wrong. I bring up the dismal healthcare system and the plight of inner-city schools. I talk about overcrowded prisons and the latest follies of the NRA. I might throw in something about elections that are won with money and companies that make a living running sweatshops. I grab whatever statistics I can. At some point, we always raise our voices. And even though I know what I'm saying is as one-sided as my father's reverie and belies the love I have for this country, I cannot stop. Of course, we aren't talking about America. At least, I'm not. All I'm talking about is being mad from all those years of him disappearing into his work, feeding his body to it and his marriage, teaching my brother and me, maybe without wanting to, that one completes the self by completing a job. It's an old story. But the fact that I now understand how the story fits together doesn't take away the anger. When it comes, it feels fresh and new, slicing through whatever calm I've been meaning to keep.

I pulled up in front of the hotel. My father climbed out of the car, his shirt still sticking to his back. "Enjoy your shower," I said. "And thanks again." He turned around and put his head back inside the car. "I had a good time," he said, and then, for a long second, he wrapped his hand around mine still holding the steering wheel. "Get some rest. Can't have the groom be tired on his wedding day." He closed the door, and I put the car in gear. I waited until my father had reached the hotel entrance, where he turned around once more and waved.

Back at the apartment Karen was busy welcoming another visitor. Sile, her bridesmaid, had arrived that afternoon and was now getting the tour of the rooms. Karen and Sile had met in graduate school and shared an apartment for three years. They hit it off right from the start, finding the same kind of humor in the habits of their professors and the juggling of footnotes, joking about this odd world they had entered, while polishing off pints of Ben & Jerry's late at night. I said hello to Sile, took my shower, and afterward sat down at my desk to check off "fix holes in barn floor" on my list.

I could hear Karen explaining the layout of the living room, telling Sile what corners to watch out for. Sile has been blind since birth. Her first task in a new apartment is to memorize the layout, and I still don't know how she does it so quickly. For a short while, her movements are tentative, her fingers reading ahead of her body, but then things fall into place, and most people who don't know she is blind can't tell the difference. She grew up on a farm in Ireland, outside of Dublin, and, like her sister and brothers, she had to do all the chores no matter how long it took. Somehow those early lessons stuck. Sile does what she wants — skiing, sailing, horseback riding — and half the time she seems more adventurous than most seeing people I know. When the three of us go to a movie together, Karen sits next to Sile and whispers an occasional update into her ear. Once, we went to see a love story together in San Francisco, a predictable Hollywood tear-jerker. Afterward, outside the theater, Sile couldn't stop laughing. "Didn't you notice?" she asked. "The cricket?" Karen and I had no idea what she was talking about. And then she told us that during the last scene, the lovers' inevitable break-up in December, a lone cricket had found its way onto the soundtrack, announcing summer in the midst of winter.

After I had updated my list of things to do, I stayed at my desk and let Karen and Sile catch up. I thought I would do some reading, but I felt too restless. My muscles were sore from working at the barn, and my mind kept going over the day I had spent with my father. I had not worked so closely with him for years. And back then it had been my father to decide on our projects, telling me what to do and how to handle the tools. Our few hours together at the barn had brought a reversal of roles, at least of a kind, and the memory of my father's eagerness to help made me feel tender, vulnerable to the confusion of love and distance that had accompanied us for so long.

I realized that I had watched my parents carefully over the last few days. I had paid close attention to my mother's left hand, the one that flutters like an unruly bird, the one she prefers to hide under the table or fix in place with her good right hand. I had noticed how quickly she tired on our walks through town, how she joked about it, blaming it on the weak American coffee. I had watched my father as well — his right eye which, with impeccable timing, turns dark red when he demands too much of himself. I had asked about his blood pressure, which he takes each morning and records in a small blue book. Sometimes he had answered me, other times he just raised his eyebrows and smiled.

Something else was different too. Helping my parents with English had become more than just routine. I had always played the interpreter when they came to visit, but this time it seemed more important to get my translations right and not cut corners. I wanted my parents involved, close by. I had no use for the silence that is part of the dance across languages. Again I went over the afternoon with my father, his earnest desire to help out, our unspoken pleasure in being together. Again I recalled my mother's labored walk and her hesitant embraces, as if she had grown reluctant to trespass on her adult son's body. I missed my parents. I knew they were nearby, sleeping eight blocks west of where I was sitting, one window open. Still I missed them. Karen's and my decision to get married, I understood, was a step into a different time and place that we would have to fill to the best of our abilities. What I hadn't considered was that our decision would also put my parents down in another place, closer to me in their joy, but also further out of reach. And it was this simple fact — our decision to marry marking time for all of us — that made me greedy for having my parents close, worrying about signs I detected of their bodies giving out, recording them with reluctant precision, as if by doing so I could contain the loss that would come.

I could hear Karen and Sile in the kitchen now, laughing, ice cubes tinkling into glasses. I thought about joining them but stayed put, kept at my desk by an unexpected question. How far would Karen and I have to travel to attend to our parents' final needs? I had no answer. All I knew was that one of us would be in another country when the time came. In that moment, our plan to stretch our lives across two continents didn't feel adventurous. It felt risky, almost foolish, filled with the subtle delay of long-distance phone calls, weeks and months watered down into e-mails and letters, and maybe, at some point, a plane caught too late when it would matter most.

On Wednesday, three days before the wedding, our list of things to do had tripled. Karen and I stayed up late to watch the weekend weather forecast. It predicted cool temperatures and rain. When my father heard about the rain, he didn't try to hide his concern. He wanted to know what our emergency plan was in case the meadow in front of the barn turned into a bog, swallowing delivery trucks and shoes. I told him there was no plan. He shook his head and came back with another question. "What about those two restrooms on the threshing floor? They don't look all that reliable to me, and you have a lot of people coming." He suggested we rent a port-a-potty, just to be on the safe side. I mentioned this idea to Karen, who mentioned it to her Aunt Elna, who said that she wouldn't be caught dead on a port-a-potty, no matter who was getting married. The good news on Wednesday came from our caterer. He told us that everything was on track, all parts of the menu lined up. "Explosions of flavor," he said, and assured us that the food Renaissance in the Midwest was still going strong.

More people kept arriving. Karen's Aunt Dorothy and Uncle Peter from Oregon, along with their daughter Carolyn. Karen's friend Joni, an opera singer from Chicago, who had volunteered to sing during the service. My brother, Andreas, and his wife, Christiane, with my nephew and niece, Felix and Annika. Friends from Germany who had bent their schedules to free up a handful of days — Bertram, Frank, Britt, Ralf, Verena, Axel, Ulf. It felt good to have them in town, dreamlike. My friends and I talked every chance we had, jumping from memories of soccer matches to my choice of wedding suit and on to Alaska, where Karen and I planned to travel next spring. There appeared to be no boundaries running through what we were saying. We talked and talked, and somehow the question of who I was in America and who I was in Germany had less room to matter. Our talks in German let me sleepwalk into Hamburg, upright and in one piece, while the town around us, the layout of its streets and buildings, the people moving through it and among them my American friends, gave proof of the life I'd lived abroad. It wasn't as if the need for translation had disappeared. Rather, there was so much translation going on at the same time — my German friends reading America and being read by it — that my own high-wire act inside of translation, for brief moments, felt like the rule, not the exception. It didn't happen all that often, just now and then, like a vista opening up you hadn't counted on finding and accept as a gift.

On Thursday, close to midnight, Bertram and Frank showed up at the apartment and dragged me out of bed. They took me to a downtown bar and after the first round of beers told me they had talked about my situation and, by and large, found it acceptable. "You may go ahead and marry Karen," Bertram said, lining his voice with the molasses-like sincerity of our fifth-grade religion teacher. They both started grinning at the same time, and then we all started laughing, drawing stares from the other tables. We stayed at the bar for another hour or so, and when they brought me back to the apartment, sleep was easy for the first time in days.

The rehearsal on Friday night went fine, not counting the fact that Mr. Bergquist stubbed his toe at the hotel and showed up forty-five minutes late. It also made us late at the restaurant, and by the time the salad was served Felix and Annika, my nephew and niece, had curled up in their seats and fallen asleep. My brother tried to feed them a few bites, which they took with eyes closed and then dozed off again. It was their first trip outside of Europe. I had told them about jet lag on the phone a couple of weeks before, and they had giggled, not quite believing me, as if I had promised them a ride on a new kind of roller coaster.

After the first course had been cleared away, my father put on his glasses, pulled a piece of paper from his pocket, and stood up. Everyone fell silent. My father coughed a couple of times and shuffled his feet. He hates speaking in front of an audience. He worries about his four years of grade school and how to usher words into sentences that are charming and witty. When I had told my father about the rehearsal dinner and that he might have to say a few words, he had looked panicked and wanted out. He took a day to think it over and finally agreed, his voice flat with surrender. Now, he was standing next to me, staring at the paper in his hands. He didn't say much, just a few sentences welcoming the guests and wishing us all a good time tonight and especially tomorrow. He wrestled with the words, trying to get his mouth to put together English well enough for people to understand. I didn't know who had helped him with the speech. Maybe the English teacher he had taken a couple of lessons from before the trip. Or maybe Helmut Godejohann, his old friend who was in town for the wedding and who had emigrated to America after the war. It didn't matter. My father spoke his words slowly and cautiously, and I listened, unable to imagine how we could fight at all.

The rest of the meal arrived with long breaks between each course. Karen and I used the extra time to hand out gifts to the bridesmaid and groomsman, Sile and my brother, and also to the four readers. Two more gifts — quilts from a nearby Amish settlement — went to our parents to thank them for their help. It was a good way of loosening things up; the gifts traveled around the tables and sparked conversations along the way. My father relaxed now that his speech was over. He and my mother were sitting across from the Bergquists. The four of them were keeping up a steady exchange of brief observations and compliments put together from English, German, smiles, and hands sketching pictures into the air. At one point, my father raised his glass. It looked as if he was getting ready for a toast, and I leaned forward to listen. My father was drinking wine, like a good many of the other guests. Since the rehearsal dinner was officially hosted by my parents, Karen and I had decided that alcohol would be in order for tonight. The Bergquists had stayed with water. My father held his glass in front of his face and with a flick of his wrist sent the wine spinning, as if getting ready to enjoy its bouquet. "Water is good," he said in English, pausing for effect, "but wine is better."

Something contracted in my stomach. The image of Mrs. Bergquist crying on our living room couch lit up in my head. I stared at my father, whose face was all fake innocence. What the hell was he thinking? Then I looked at Mrs. Bergquist. I thought it possible she might leave the table or maybe set my father straight with a remark of her own. She didn't. Instead, she smiled, ignoring my father as if he had just floated his tie in the soup, the kind of thing you choose not to notice to keep the other person from looking like a fool. I leaned back in my chair. Gradually, my stomach unclenched. I felt a rush of gratitude toward Mrs. Bergquist, her graciousness in the face of my father's leaden humor, and I wondered how else she might surprise me in the future.

The gifts were still being handed around. Dessert and coffee appeared on the table. Felix and Annika lay curled up in their chairs, breathing regularly, oblivious of everything. When dinner ended, my brother tried to shake his son and daughter awake. It took a while for them to open their eyes, and as soon as the shaking stopped they were out again. Finally, my brother picked up Annika in her sleep. I leaned down to Felix to do the same. I slipped my arms under him but couldn't find the right position. Each time I started lifting, Felix's muscles turned liquid and he slipped back into the chair. He was a lot heavier than I remembered from a year ago, when I had played with him last.

In the end, I got him to sit up and open his eyes. He stared at me for a long moment, trying to focus — the face of his uncle, his father's brother, who was getting married in a place that brought on sleep like lightning. I pulled him to his feet. He wrapped his arms around me, buried his face in my stomach, and let me drag him after my brother, down the stairs, into the taxi already waiting outside.

Twenty minutes before the service, I'm alone in the minister's office. I'm dressed in a blue three-piece suit, pacing back and forth, stopping in front of the window every other minute or so to see who is arriving. Either nobody is showing up, or everyone is coming in from Gilbert Street, outside my field of vision. I debate whether to push my face against the window to get a better angle, but then decide it would be too embarrassing to be seen like that. So far, the day has gone okay. I spent the morning at the barn, helping to unload chairs and tables. Then I came back to the apartment, took a shower, and spent forty minutes grinding coffee that will be served with petit fours after the service. Karen was already gone. She spent last night with her family at the hotel, and I will not see her until she steps next to me in front of Jason, our minister.

After I was done grinding coffee, Bertram stopped by to check up on me and take me to church. I think he is having a good time on his first visit to America. But I know he would enjoy it even more if his wife could be along. Ionara is from Brazil, and she forgot to apply for a visa on time, which did little to improve her opinion of America. I was putting on my suit when Bertram arrived. He told me it looked good, which he had to say, of course. I let him straighten my tie and pull the suit here and there until he was satisfied. Bertram has always been a sharp dresser. Suits and shirts cling to him with careless elegance, which has as much to do with his taste as with his body. In high school, he put all of us to shame in P.E. class, outjumping and outrunning us at will in whatever sport he chose. We didn't admit it back then, but his was the body we tried to catch up with. And even this morning, when he tucked me into shape for my wedding, some of his high school authority was still there, and I gave in to it, eager to make the team.

There is a knock on the door. Jason peeks inside and tells me it's time. I walk out into the narthex, where the procession has lined up — Karen's cousin Carolyn at the front, holding the cross, followed by the acolytes and the choir in rows of two. Then my brother and Sile. When I take my place behind them, my brother looks over his shoulder and tries to wink, which tells me he is as nervous as I am. Sile turns her head sideways, listening to my footsteps on the carpet. I know that Karen must be standing behind me now, and I know that I cannot turn around. I have not seen her dress or the headpiece she is wearing, which her grandmother wore in 1934, when she married a Swedish immigrant in her uncle's garden in Los Angeles.

Before Karen moved back to Iowa from California, her grandmother had given us a farewell party at her house in Sacramento. She cooked a mountain of food, spreading it out on her large dining room table. In the middle of the table she placed a cake with our names on it and two figurines, bride and groom, the decoration from her own wedding cake. At first I couldn't tell why the bride and groom looked unusual. It wasn't just the old-fashioned cut of the couple's clothes. It was something more basic. I looked again. The groom was naked from his waist down to his shoes, the bride from her shoulders down to her stomach. Seventy years of traveling through fingers had stripped them of their finery.

The music starts up, and the procession moves forward. The church is not empty. Everyone did come in from Gilbert Street. I have the service program in the inside pocket of my jacket. All the places where Karen and I get up or sit down or do anything at all are marked. I'm trying to walk slowly, but not too slowly; my goal is to make it to the end of the aisle at a dignified pace, not sluggish or stiff, something in between, which I manage quite well for a few steps, I think, and then

Karen is next to me, and I can't figure out how it is that we are alone in this church, Jason and the others looking on, and not alone at the same time. I forget the service program and the places marked. I forget my body inside a blue three-piece suit. I forget what separates my brother's hand holding out the rings from the song Joni is singing from the words John is reading in English, then Bertram in German.

Karen and I are the first to take Communion. We watch as our parents make their way to the altar, followed by most of the other guests, a steady line filing past us and seeking out our faces. They smile at us. Some nod ever so slightly, others wink, two or three try on a mask of mock surprise. The longer Communion takes, the more I want this irregular procession to continue. In our brief encounters, I feel I'm being handed something solid, something I can stack inside the questions I have about what will come. Not answers, exactly, but bits of lives lived, some in Germany and some in America, part of the fabric out of which Karen and I will have to put together a space that can contain us. The faces keep coming. Karen's brother, Paul, and his wife, JoAnn, who live on the shore of Lake Michigan. My friend Ulf who builds houses in Hamburg. Steve who once studied in my hometown and has settled in Texas, a father of four. Axel who teaches law in Würzburg. Don and Janet who farm in the San Joaquin Valley. Britt who practices medicine in Harburg. My father's friend Helmut who left Germany in 1957, who now lives in Wisconsin and speaks his native language inside the melody of another. Clarice. Andreas. John. Verena. Christi. Frank. Tim. Annegret. Kara. Kotoka. Susan. Christiane. Joe.

They are all in front of the church now. Waiting for us to come out. Through the glass door I can see the black 1930s Chevy that will take us to the barn. My father and his friend Helmut are standing at the curb, listening to the driver, his hand drawing circles in the air above the hood. We push open the door and start down the stairs. The first handfuls of birdseed are raining down on us, finding their way into my hair and collar. At the bottom of the stairs are Karen's nephews, Patrick and David, and Felix is right next to them. They all have their birdseed cones ready to go, and the last thing I see before I close my eyes is the three of them moving forward like a row of linemen, and then birdseed is everywhere, on my lips, in my ears, and more of it down my collar, where it trickles past my shoulder blades and collects somewhere above my belt. I imagine the birdseed getting caught in Karen's headpiece and in her long, sleeveless dress. I imagine she has her eyes closed, too.

During the first warm stretch of May, eight months later, Karen and I walked through the rooms of our apartment, trying to figure out what to take with us to Germany and what to leave behind. A few times we quarreled about particular attachments — Karen's old high school blow-dryer going up against my eight-dollar 1965 Encyclopedia Britannica — but in the end we managed to agree. We stacked everything we would take in the living room and then ushered our friends through the rest of the apartment, encouraging them to pick what they could use and raid our spices. We also held a garage sale, which netted us some two hundred dollars but still left us with a Macintosh Classic and three potted plants. We took several carloads of our belongings to the Salvation Army, the place humming with end-of-school-year business. Whatever else there was we stuffed into trash bags, which soon covered our garage floor from one end to the other and which our landlady agreed to dispose of in manageable quantities.

What made our packing still more complicated was the fact that we had scheduled a two-week trip to Alaska right before our departure for Germany. It was our honeymoon, which had had to wait while I was finishing up school — seven months of disappearing behind stacks of books and getting forgetful about showers. The day before the movers came to pick up our overseas shipment, Karen suggested we take a final trip out to the barn. We had been planning to do so for a while, saving the last bottle of sparkling cider from the reception and also a handful of frozen petit fours. It was a pleasant day for the drive along Highway 6, the late afternoon sun sharpening the lines of fields and roads. As I had done on previous trips, I kept my eye out for a yellow two-story house that stood near the highway, not far from where we had to turn onto a gravel road. It had become a kind of landmark, a place I kept waiting for and that made me turn my head each time I passed by.

A year ago, at the end of May, a tornado had touched down east of town and cut across Highway 6. I had watched its path on the TV weather map, shaking my head in disbelief because the storm was heading straight for the barn. The next day I drove out to see what had happened, and that was when the yellow two-story house first settled in my memory. Its roof had been ripped open. All the windows were gone, the front porch razed and pushed into a pile of rubble. Two grain silos standing next to the house had been torn apart; their pieces covered the yard like oversize tinfoil. The trees lining the driveway had been reduced to a row of scarred, splintered stumps. The last thing I saw, driving by, was a man and woman standing next to a pickup truck near the end of the driveway, taking in what the storm had done. When I reached the barn, I didn't even bother to turn off the engine. I jumped out of the car and circled the entire structure, checking and rechecking. Everything was fine. Not a single board out of place. Somewhere in the half mile between house and barn, the storm must have turned or slipped back into the sky or done whatever to disappear.

"The house is coming up," I said to Karen, who was busy leafing through our Alaska guidebook, marking hikes she had taken years ago when her family had lived in Anchorage. She had ambitious plans for filling me in on the places she remembered. I kept looking for the house to show up on my left. It sat on a slight hill about a hundred yards from the road, easy to spot. The last time I had seen it, most of the rubble had been cleared away. It had looked as if the owners were getting ready to put the place back together. There was one more drawn-out curve to the right, a patch of oak trees next to an old windmill, then the hill. The house was gone. Not even the driveway was visible anymore. The hill was a clear green line against the sky. For a moment, I was too surprised to speak, and then I started thinking of our apartment in town, the place half-empty, the living room floor covered with everything we owned. I thought of the movers who would pack our belongings the next day, leaving us with five suitcases, a backpack, and two plane tickets to Germany. I imagined our arrival in Hamburg, the blur of the first few weeks — the countless forms to fill out for Karen's residency permit and work papers; phone calls and letters to find me a job; the chance of having to move again, another city, another apartment, somewhere. All I could find to think about was motion. And in the midst of that rush, the disappearance of the house affected me like vertigo. I hated the idea that it could vanish like that, because it seemed possible, just then, to see it as a hint of what might be in store for us — places of residence, convenient and temporary, not one of them strong enough to withstand the insistent tug of two countries.

I steered the car around the next curve. Karen was still reading the guidebook. Two years ago, Karen and I had spent a summer in Hamburg, and now, with my mind skipping like a stone across water, the memory of that trip was inside the car as well. We had moved into a small apartment in my parents' house, which had worked out fairly well, apart from my mother's habit of leaving bags of food outside our door. Within a few days, we had more cake and fruit than anyone could eat, and we didn't have the heart to complain. Both Karen and I had brought along work, but we still had time to look around, taking trips to Cologne, Amsterdam, and Berlin, a city Karen found cold and uninviting. She told me that she liked Hamburg better, which made me an even more enthusiastic guide, dragging her to the downtown sights — St. Michaelis Kirche, Rathaus, Alsterarkaden, Speicherstadt — and then through my old neighborhood. I showed her Bramfelder Lake, where my friends and I would skate in the winter, and I took her to the tennis courts in Farmsen, where I had hung out in the summer.

One night, a few weeks into our stay, I had given her a tour of my grade school on Hegholt. I had walked her from one end of the schoolyard to the other, describing our elaborate chases and pointing out trees we used to raid for crab apples. As usual, Karen and I spoke English, and I kept piling up the stories to give her something to see. But the more I talked, the more awkward I felt. It had rained that morning, and all I could notice as I was pulling out my stories was the same wet asphalt smell coming off the schoolyard. It was the visceral blow of being in a childhood place. A recognition that required no words. And yet, it was words I kept using, English words, that soon hovered so far above the ground that they brought nothing into focus — not the games the children had played, nor the boy who had moved among them inside German.

It had rained a lot during our time in Germany. Weeks of gray skies and drizzle that I had ignored at first, and then took as a personal insult. Karen and I hadn't yet talked about getting married, but the idea was in the back of our minds. We had a quiet understanding that our stay in Hamburg was a kind of test to find out how the two of us would fare in my country. And it was because of this unspoken agreement that I began to argue with the clouds and the drizzle like a man not quite in control of his faculties. Between complaints about the weather, we kept visiting with friends and family. They all were curious to hear how Karen liked her stay, and even though I soon knew what she would say — Yes, she liked it very well, although, of course, it was too early to know for sure — I never stopped listening to her answers with a hint of nervousness. Karen had studied German in college for several years, and more than once she impressed everyone with the words she pulled out when the questions started coming. She received lots of compliments on her skills, and each time her face would light up with a mix of pleasure and surprise.

About two months into our stay, we were getting ready to attend a party downtown. The hosts were old friends of mine, who had asked me not too long ago to be the godfather of their second daughter. Most of the other guests would be friends too, some from as far back as high school, and I was looking forward to our conversations over good food. I finished getting dressed and then went into the bedroom to see whether Karen was ready as well. She sat on the edge of our bed and didn't look up when I came in. "Are you okay?" I asked. I sat down next to her, and when she turned her head I could see that she was trembling. "What is it?" I put my arm around her. She didn't say anything for a while. But then, haltingly, she started to talk about how nervous she was about the party, about seeing my friends, some of whom she had already met. She liked them, she said, and she wanted them to like her as well, which was exactly the problem, because how was this supposed to work if all she had was German, which kept stealing what she was thinking, her observations, her ways of being funny, her courtesy and consideration, which kept taking away who she was and wanted to be.

"It takes time," I had said, startled to see my friends turn into complete strangers. "Don't be so hard on yourself. It just takes a lot of time." I wanted to find something else to say. I wanted to sound more eloquent and consoling, but I couldn't, because I knew what she was talking about. I had felt it on my own skin more often than I cared to remember. "It just takes time," I had said again, which was true, of course. But it was also a lie, because the gap Karen wanted to close, I knew, wouldn't yield completely. And then I had hugged her hard, wondering whether we could lose each other.

The grass in front of the barn had grown high enough to brush against the bottom of the car as we pulled up. We pushed open the sliding door and started climbing the stairs to the hayloft. The place looked like it did the first time when I had stopped by more or less on a fluke. Big wooden tables stood scattered around the loft, lined with an assortment of wood, metal, and plastic chairs. The stack of rotting hay bales was sitting back in the northwest corner, and the hay-chutes once again sported their "Do Not Climb" signs. A few of our extension cords and clamp lamps were still around. We had asked the owner whether he could use them, and he had been glad to accept. "Check it out," Karen said. "Still works." She was standing at the edge of the hayloft, her hand resting on a simple wooden gate she and I had built to keep our nieces and nephews from falling. I nodded and began to scan the floor, looking for the small pieces of wood my father and I put in. I found most of them, a roughly cut collection of squares and triangles, riddled with more screws than I remembered using.

We sat down at one of the tables, poured some of the cider into plastic cups, and divided up the petit fours. Part of the table was still wet from last night's rain, which had blown in through the open cupola windows. A day before the wedding, Karen and I had decided to keep those cupola windows closed because of the bad weather that had been forecast. It had been a smart thing to do, but somehow we didn't get any rain. Instead, the temperature had climbed into the high eighties, and the hot and humid air in the barn had nowhere to go. For the first hour or so of the reception, hardly anyone ventured inside. We all stood in front of the barn in small groups, glad to catch the evening breeze that had sprung up. But then it was time for the opening dance, and everyone came up to the hayloft to watch Karen and me two-step as the band started into the song we had played in our kitchen at night. I counted the beat and still managed to step on Karen's toes. Our parents joined us after a while, all of us slowly spinning in the heat. Several people circled the dance floor with cameras, among them Karen's Aunt Elna, who was eager to get a picture of Mrs. Bergquist dancing, a prospect that made her shake her head and giggle. I kept counting the beat. Occasionally, I caught a glimpse of the buffet table whose centerpiece, a four-tier frosted carrot cake, had begun to slant.

The heat hadn't let up until the owner of the barn stopped by after dinner. He offered to climb up the reverse ladder to the cupola and open the windows. It was a difficult, nerve-wracking climb, which Karen and I had tried only once months earlier. Everyone had watched as the owner made his way up to the cupola on all fours, negotiating the uneven spaces between the rungs. After he had left, the barn cooled down quickly. The band, still tired from last night's gig, hit its stride, and the dance floor stayed full for the rest of the evening. My mother and father were out there with their friends Helmut and Chris, dancing and reminiscing at the same time. Bertram, who is a good dancer, shared his ballroom expertise with Britt and Verena and Sile and Kotoka and also talked Mrs. Bergquist into another try. For a while, my brother and his wife fought their jet lag and kept up with everyone else. Karen and I danced right in front of the band. I was happy to have survived the opening two-step, to stop counting the beat, and whenever someone cut in to dance with Karen, her brothers Paul and John or somebody else, I watched them spin her around with a silly, incredulous smile.

Karen and I didn't have far to go after the reception. We had rented a room in a local bed & breakfast just a few streets from our apartment. When we arrived, we were too wound up to think about sleep and too exhausted to think about anything else. We stretched out on the polished hardwood floor, staring at the ceiling and going over the day. Slowly and without order, we passed the day back and forth like pictures. When we got too tired, we stood up and began undressing. I slipped out of my jacket, and even before it was completely off, I could hear the birdseed raining down on the hardwood floor. There was more of it when I took off my shirt, and still more as Karen got out of her gown. We continued to undress, stopping every few seconds to hear the seed murmuring across the floor, small waves heading for the bed and the dresser and the couch, until we stood in front of each other, naked, both familiar and new.

Karen finished her cup of cider, brushed away the crumbs from the petit fours, and stood up from the table. We took another look around the hayloft, then climbed down to the threshing floor. It was dark enough outside to drive back to town with our headlights on. Dark enough to keep me from searching for the yellow two-story house. Instead, I kept my eyes on the road, watching it unfurl, turn solid, and slip away.

Sightline Books

The Iowa Series in Literary Nonfiction

Embalming Mom: Essays in Life

JANET BURROWAY

No Such Country: Essays toward Home

ELMAR LUETH